Handy English

Encoder
Decoder

ALSO BY HARVEY BLUEDORN

A Greek Alphabetarion, 1993

*Vocabulary Bridges from English to Latin
& Greek*, 1994

*Homeschool Greek: A Thorough Self-
Teaching Grammar of Biblical Greek*,
1996

*Teaching the Trivium: Christian
Homeschooling in a Classical Style*,
2001

*Ancient History from Primary Sources: A
Literary Timeline*, 2003

Handy English
Encoder
Decoder

ALL THE SPELLING
AND PHONICS RULES
YOU COULD EVER
WANT TO KNOW

by Harvey Bluedorn

SECOND EDITION
MAY 2004
TRIVIUM PURSUIT

Handy English Encoder Decoder
by Harvey Bluedorn

Library of Congress Control Number: 2003098219
ISBN 0-9743616-2-3

Trivium Pursuit
PMB 168, 429 Lake Park Blvd.
Muscatine, Iowa 52761
309-537-3641
www.triviumpursuit.com

"Thou shalt not muzzle the ox that treadeth out the corn. And, The labourer is worthy of his reward." – 1 Timothy 5:18

" 'Therefore, behold, I am against the prophets,' saith the LORD, 'that steal my words every one from his neighbour.' " – Jeremiah 23:30

"...Thou shalt not steal." – Romans 13:9

"That no man go beyond and defraud his brother in any matter: because that the Lord is the avenger of all such, as we also have forewarned you and testified." – 1 Thessalonians 4:6

Contents
OF THIS BOOK

Appendices

Introduction
ABOUT THIS BOOK

Good spellers (encoders) are usually good readers (de-coders); but good readers are not necessarily good spell-ers. Many persons of large intelligence who read well and who read widely are nevertheless very poor spellers. Though some persons seem to be natural-born spell-ers, nearly anyone who applies diligence to learning the general spelling rules and who consults his dictionary regularly can be a good speller.

Phonics rules help spelling and spelling rules help phonics. For example, if we know the spelling rule that no word can end with the letter j, and the phonics rule that g does not make the (soft) "j" sound unless it is followed by e, i, or y, then we know that a word which sounds phonetically like "rāj" must end with g and silent e (another spelling rule). It cannot end with dge unless the vowel before it is short (another spelling rule). There-fore it is probably spelled rage.

From many sources, old and new, we have compiled a brief but comprehensive list of spelling and phonics rules. This book is not a full-fledged spelling or phonics program. Rather, it is a handbook which may be used as a ready reference tool by itself, or it may be used as a resource tool in conjunction with a spelling or a phonics curriculum. Two spelling games and a phonics game are given in the Appendices, along with an exhaustive list of homophones (words which are pronounced the same but are spelled differently).

Encoder
SPELLING RULES

1. Of Words in General

1.1   A *primitive word* is a word which cannot be re-
      duced to any simpler word (man, good, content).
      A *derivative word* is one which may be reduced
      to another simpler word in English (*man*ful,
      *good*ness, *content*ment).

1.2   There are many words which are *primitives*
      in English but which are *derivatives* in other
      languages, such as Latin (circum-spect, de-lude,
      con-cave, com-plicate).

2. Dictionary Rules of Syllable Division

These are the rules for syllable division commonly employed in English dictionaries. Sometimes they are not the same as the natural division of syllables in common speech. Those natural divisions are listed later in the Decoder (phonics) section of this book.

2.1   A single consonant between two vowels is joined to the second vowel.
• de-light, bri-dal, re-source

EXCEPTION: The letter x, and compound words.
• ex-ist, ex-amine, up-on, un-even, dis-ease

2.2   Two consonants together, and which cannot begin a word (tm, nd, ff, etc.), and which are between two vowels, must be divided.
• ut-most, un-der, in-sect, er-ror, cof-fin

2.3   Two consonants which blend together (bl, cr, dw, etc.), and which can begin a word, and which are between two vowels – the first of which is clearly long – must not be separated.
• fa-ble, sti-fle, re-gret, pro-gram, re-place, re-close
• prog-ress, rep-resent, rec-luse (The first vowel is short, so they can be separated.)

2.4   Three consonants in the middle of a word, and which can begin a word, if the preceding vowel is long, must not be separated.
• de-throne, de-stroy

2.5   When there are three consonants in the middle of a word, and which can begin a word, if the preceding vowel is short, one of the consonants

always belongs to the preceding syllable.
• dis-tract, dis-prove

2.6 When three or four consonants which cannot begin a word are between two vowels, such consonants as can begin a syllable belong to the latter syllable, the rest to the former syllable.
• ab-stain, com-plete, em-broil, dan-dler, ap-ple, con-strain, hand-some, parch-ment

2.7 Two vowels together must be divided into separate syllables, unless they form a diphthong (vowel blend ai, au, ei, eu, oi, ou).
• cru-el, deni-al, soci-ety

2.8 Compounded words are divided into the simple words from which they are composed.
• ice-house, over-power, never-the-less

2.9 Grammatical suffixes, and other word endings, are generally separated.
• teach-er, teach-es, teach-ing, wretch-ed, free-dom, great-er, great-est

3. Vowel Rules

3.1 ei may begin a word, but not end a word. ie may end a word, but not begin a word.
• eight, tie

3.2 When representing the long "e" sound, spell ie, except when following c or when representing another vowel sound (usually long "a" sound), then spell ei. [Rhyming version: i before e, except after c; or when sounded like a, as in neighbor and weigh.]

- believe, chief, thief, thievery, yield, niece, siege, series (long "e" sound spelled ie)
- ceiling, conceit, receipt, deceive (long "e" sound spelled ei after c)
- vein, reign, eight, neighbor (long "a" sound spelled ei)
- foreign, sovereign, forfeit, counterfeit (short "i" sound spelled ei)
- height, Fahrenheit, meiosis, seismic, stein (long "i" sound spelled ei)
- heifer (short "e" sound spelled ei)

EXCEPTION: When the two vowels are pronounced separately.
- atheist, deist, reinforce
- science, piety, quiet

EXCEPTION: When y has been changed to i in order to add a suffix, keep ie even after c.
- agency—agencies, fancy—fancied

EXCEPTION: When ci represents the "sh" sound.
- sufficient, efficient, conscience

EXCEPTION: Established spellings.
- either, neither, seize, seizure, leisure, caffeine, codeine, protein, weird (long "e" sound spelled ei)
- financier, species (long "e" sound is spelled ie after c)
- friend, mischief, review (ie does not represent the long "e" sound)

3.3   y not i, w not u, is used at the end of an English word.
- (ay, ey, oy, uy, aw, ew, ow, but not ai, ei, oi, ui, au, eu, ou) say, obey, boy, buy, paw, pew

EXCEPTION:
- taxi is short for taxicab.
- macaroni is an Italian word.
- you, thou
- caribou and other foreign words

4. Consonant Rules

4.1   The "j" sound can be spelled by:

4.1.1   j except at the end of a word.
- jam, jelly, jig, jog, jug

4.1.2   g when followed by e , i, or y.
- ginger, gym

4.1.3   dge after a short vowel at the end of a primitive word, or dg before a suffix.
- badge, edge, bridge, dodge, judgement or judgment

4.1.4   di after l or r.
- soldier, cordial

4.1.5   d followed by u.
- educate, schedule, gradual.

4.2   The "k" sound can be spelled by:

4.2.1   k almost anywhere.
- Kate, lake, key, seek, kite, hike, kook, kudos, Luke

4.2.2   ck after a short vowel.
- păck, pĕck, pĭck, pŏck, pŭck

4.2.3   ch except at the end of a word.
- chasm, anchor

4.2.4   che at the end of a word.
- ache

4.2.5   q except at the end of a word.
- quest, banquet

4.2.6   que at the end of a word.
- antique

4.3   The "s" sound can be spelled by:

4.3.1   s almost anywhere.
- sat, ask, set, best, sit, list, son, cost, sun, dust

4.3.2   c followed by e, i, or y.
- cent, cinder, cycle

4.3.3   ss after a short vowel ending a syllable.
- glass, confess, kiss, boss, fuss

4.3.4   sc when followed by e, i, or y.
- scene, scientist, scythe

4.3.5   se at the end of a word.
- case, geese, vise, close, use

4.4   The "ks" sound can be spelled by:

4.4.1   cks after a short vowel ending a word.
- păcks, pĕcks, pĭcks, pŏcks, pŭcks

4.4.2   kes after a long vowel ending a word.
- bākes, bīkes, cōkes, dūkes

4.4.3   chs at the end of a word.
- Bachs

4.4.4   cc followed by e or i.
- access, accident

4.4.5   x or xc almost anywhere (except the beginning of a word).
 • box, except

4.5   The "ng" sound of **gang** can be spelled by:

4.5.1   ng at the end of a word or when not followed by a long vowel.
 • gang, singer

4.5.2   n when followed by a palatal g, k, ch, or x. (Note: g is pronounced separately in **anger**.)
 • anger, ink, anchor, lynx

4.6   g used to say "j" or c used to say "s" must be followed by e, i, or y.
 • pigeon, religious, energy
 • cent, city, cypress

4.7   -dge may be used only after a single short vowel.
 • bădge, ĕdge, rĭdge, lŏdge, jŭdge

4.8   In order to preserve the hard sound of c, words which end with hard c will add k before a suffix beginning with e, i, or y.
 • frolic—frolicked, frolicking, frolicky

4.9   ck may be used only after a single short vowel.
 • păck, pĕck, pĭck, pŏck, pŭck

4.10   q is almost always followed by u.
 • quiz, acquire

 EXCEPTION:
 • Iraq

4.11   s never immediately follows x. There is an "s" sound already in x, "ks." However, a c followed by e or i can be used immediately after an x.
 • excess, excite

4.12   sh may be used at the end of a syllable, but never at the beginning of a syllable, except at the

beginning of a word.
- shall, fish, finish

EXCEPTION: The ending -ship.
- friendship, worship, hardship

4.13　si, su, ti, ci are the spellings most frequently used to say "sh" or "zh" when beginning a syllable, but not when beginning a word.
- mansion, vision, measure, nation, vicious

4.14　ch, ti, tu, tch are the spellings most frequently used to say the "tch" sound.
- church, fraction, situate, itch

4.15　The letters h, j, k, q, v, w, x, y are never doubled.
- show—showing, box—boxed, pay—paying

4.16　The letters b, d, f, g, l, m, n, p, s are regularly doubled between vowels when the first vowel is short.
- bagger, daddy, fluffy, lollipop, mommy, nanny, pepper, sassy

4.17　The "f" sound can be spelled by:

4.17.1　f almost anywhere.
- farfetched

4.17.2　ff between vowels, or at the end of a word.
- puffin, puff

4.17.3　ph in words of Greek origin.
- phosphor

4.17.4　gh at the end of some primitive words.
- rough

4.18　z (never s) is used to say "z" at the beginning of a word.
- zebra, zoo

EXCEPTION: x also says the "z" sound at the beginning of a word, but not elsewhere.
• xenon, xenophobia, xerography, xylophone

5. Suffix Rules

5.1 Words ending in -y

5.1.1 If a word ends in -y preceded by a vowel, then keep the y when adding a suffix.
• day—days, attorney—attorneys, annoy—annoyance, enjoy—enjoyment, play—played

EXCEPTION: Five English words ending in -y preceded by an a have established spellings which change y to i.
• lay—laid, pay—paid, say—said, slay—slain, day—daily

5.1.2 If a word ends in -y preceded by a consonant or qu, then change the y to i before adding a suffix.
• happy—happily—happiness, likely—likelihood, industry—industrious, soliloquy—soliloquies

EXCEPTION: To avoid double i, retain the y before suffixes beginning with i.
• try—tried, but trying; baby—babies, but babyish

EXCEPTION: Retain the y before the suffix -ness after some one-syllable words.
• shyness, spryness, dryness, shyness

EXCEPTION: Established spellings retaining the y.
• babyhood

EXCEPTION: The possessive suffix -'s.
• baby—babies—baby's

EXCEPTION: y sometimes changes to e before a suffix beginning with a vowel.
• bounty—bounteous, duty—duteous, beauty—beauteous, pity—piteous, plenty—plenteous

5.2   Words ending in -fy

5.2.1   Most words ending in -fy change y to i and take -cation.
• deify—deification, fortify—fortification

EXCEPTION: A few words drop y and take -action.
• stupefy—stupefaction, putrefy—putrefaction

5.3   Words ending in -ie

5.3.1   Words ending in -ie change those letters to y before a suffix beginning with i.
• die—dying, tie—tying, vie—vying, belie—belying

5.4   Words ending in -able/-ible

5.4.1   Nouns ending in -ation have adjective forms which end in -able.
• application—applicable, fortification—fortifiable

EXCEPTION: Some nouns which do not have an -ation form do take an -able ending.
• adjustable, comfortable, desirable, erasable, livable, remarkable

5.4.2 Nouns ending in -ce or -ge which have adjective forms which end in -able retain the e before adding -able in order to keep the c or g soft.
• embrace—embraceable, exchange—exchangeable

5.4.3 Adjectives ending in -ible often have noun forms which end in -tion (not -ation) or -sion, and often have stems which end in -ss.
• destruction—destructible, corruption—corruptible, digestion—digestible, exhaustion—exhaustible, suggestion—suggestible
• comprehension—comprehensible, persuasion—persuasible
• accession—accessible, permission—permissible

5.4.4 Stems which end with soft c in -uce or with soft g in -igent take an -ible ending in order to keep the c or g soft.
• produce—producible, deduce—deducible
• intelligent—intelligible, negligent—negligible

EXCEPTION: Some nouns which do not have a -tion or -sion ending, or stems which end in -ss or -uce or -igent, do take an -ible ending.
• eligible, incorrigible

5.5 Words ending in silent -e

5.5.1 Silent e at the end of a word is usually dropped before a suffix beginning with a vowel, but is kept before a suffix beginning with a consonant.
• care—caring—careless, late—later—lately, name—naming—nameless, like—likable—likely, locate—located—location, use—used—usable

EXCEPTION: Words ending in -ce and -ge retain e before suffixes beginning with -a or -o (-able and -ous) in order to keep the c or g soft. See

5.4.4.
- peace—peaceable, courage—courageous

EXCEPTION: Words ending in -oe or -ee usually retain the e unless the suffix begins with e. See 5.5.1
- hoe—hoeing—hoed,
canoe—canoeing—canoed,
free—freeing—freed

EXCEPTION: Words ending in -ue usually drop the -e when the suffix begins with a consonant.
- true—truly, due—duly, argue—argument

EXCEPTION: Words ending in -dge sometimes drop -e in American English.
- judgment or judgement
- acknowledgment or acknowledgement
- abridgment or abridgement

EXCEPTION: Some words retain final -e to distinguish them from similar words.
- dye—dyeing (vs. die—dying),
singe—singeing (vs. sing—singing)

EXCEPTION: Established spellings.
- awe—awful (but awesome), whole—wholly (but wholesome), nine—ninth (but nineteen), mile—mileage, acre—acreage

5.5.2   Many words ending in -ize drop e and take -ation.
- legalize—legalization, civilize—civilization

5.5.3   Some words not ending in -ize also take -ation.
- sense—sensation, form—formation, inflame—inflammation

5.5.4   Many words ending in -ate drop the te before adding an ending.
- estimate—estimable, agitate—agitable, accurate—accuracy, delicate—delicacy

5.5.5 Words ending in -cede, -ceed, -sede: -cede is the common ending.
- concede, precede, recede, secede

EXCEPTION: Only three words end in -ceed.
- exceed, proceed, succeed

EXCEPTION: One word ends in -sede.
- supersede

5.6 Words ending in a consonant

5.6.1 A word of one syllable, which ends in f, l, or s preceded by a single vowel, doubles the final consonant.
- off, staff, ill, mill, pass, roll, will, bass, boss, glass

EXCEPTION:
- as, bus, gal, gas, gel, has, his, if, is, nil, of, pal, this, thus, us, was, yes (These are the only exceptions.)

5.6.2 A word of one syllable, which ends with any consonant except f, l, or s, preceded by a single vowel, never doubles the final consonant.
- bob, dad, leg, mom, hop, jar, sit

EXCEPTION:
- ebb, add, odd, egg, inn, bunn, err, purr, butt, buzz

5.6.3 A word of one syllable, which ends in a single consonant preceded by a single short vowel, doubles that final consonant before a suffix beginning with a vowel, or before the suffix -y.
- hit—hitting, drop—dropped, big—biggest, mud—muddy

CONTRASTING EXAMPLES:
- help—helping (because it ends in two consonants)

• need—needing—needy (because the final consonant is preceded by two vowels)

EXCEPTION:
• gas—gaseous

5.6.4   A word of more than one syllable, which accents the last syllable, and which ends in a single consonant preceded by a single vowel, doubles the final consonant when adding a suffix beginning with a vowel.
• begin—beginning, admit—admitting—admitted

CONTRASTING EXAMPLES:
• enter—entered (because the accent is not on the last syllable)
• civil—civilian (because the accent is not on the last syllable in the primitive, even though it is in the derivative)
• toil—toiling (because the consonant is preceded by two vowels)
• gild—gilded (because it ends with two consonants)

EXCEPTION: If the accent is shifted away from the last syllable when the suffix is added.
• confer—conferring—conference

EXCEPTION: Sometimes in forming the derivative, one of the vowels is dropped, so the consonant is doubled.
• appeal—appellant, fail—fallible

5.6.5   Words ending in dd, ff, ll, or ss retain the double consonant when forming derivatives.
• odd—oddness, stiff—stiffness, call—calling, hiss—hissing

EXCEPTION: Words ending in ll followed by a suffix beginning with a consonant drop one l.
• full—ful-ness—ful-ly, skill—skil-less—skil-ful

5.6.6   A verb ending in er or ur, which accents the last syllable, doubles the r in the past tense.
• occur—occurred, prefer—preferred

5.6.7   A verb ending in er, which does not accent the last syllable, does not double the r in the past tense.
• answer—answered, offer—offered, dif-fer—differed

5.6.8   Simple words ending in ll, when joined to another word and retaining their accent, retain the ll. If they lose their accent, they drop one l.
• ful-fill, will-ful, fore-tell, aw-ful, hope-ful, hand-ful, al-ready

EXCEPTION:
• un-til, wel-come, al-ways, al-so, with-al

5.7   Plurals

5.7.1   Add -s to singular nouns (including proper nouns) to form the plural.
• bugs, skis, bones

EXCEPTION: Add -es to singular nouns (including proper nouns) ending in a sibilant ("s"-like) sound, such as: soft ch, s, ss, sh, tch, ts, x, z, or tz.
• marches, Joneses, bosses, marshes, matches, boxes, buzzes, Fritzes

EXCEPTION: Add -es to words with the final y changed to i. (See 5.1.)
• baby—babies, fly—flies

5.7.2   Most nouns ending in -f or -fe change to -ves in the plural form.
• leaf—leaves, knife—knives, wife—wives, beef—beeves, calf—calves, self—selves, thief—thieves

EXCEPTION: Some nouns ending in -f or -fe add s to form the plural.

- puff—puffs, fife—fifes, chief—chiefs, handkerchief—handkerchiefs, roof—roofs, dwarf—dwarfs (or dwarves)

5.7.3 Some plurals are irregular simply because of their foreign origins.

- Greek words: analysis—analyses, thesis—theses, antithesis—antitheses, synthesis—syntheses, crisis—crises
- Latin words: alumnus—alumni, bacillus—bacilli, bacterium—bacteria, datum—data, erratum—errata, larva—larvae, species—species
- Old English words: child—children, ox—oxen, man—men, woman—women, tooth—teeth, goose—geese, mouse—mice, moose—moose, sheep—sheep, deer—deer

EXCEPTION: Some Greek and Latin words have alternate English plurals.

- Greek words: criterion—criteria or criterions, phenomenon—phenomena or phenomenons
- Latin words: appendix—appendices or appendixes, curriculum—curricula or curriculums, medium—media or mediums, memorandum—memoranda or memorandums, radius—radii or radiuses

5.7.4 Never use an apostrophe to form the plural of a word, a capitalized acronym, or a year date. (The apostrophe is reserved for possessives and contractions.)

- ETOAs, VIPs, 1960s

EXCEPTION: Plurals of letters, numbers, signs, abbreviations, or specific words being discussed, where there might be confusion.

- A's & B's, ABC's, 6's, #'s, @'s, Ph.D.'s, too many the's

5.7.5 Words ending in i or o, and preceded by a consonant, generally form plurals with -es. (But consult your dictionary.)
• echoes, heroes, tomatoes, potatoes

EXCEPTION:
• autos, photos, pianos, radios, solos
• buffalo (collectively) or buffaloes or buffalos, dominoes or dominos, volcanoes or volcanos

5.7.6 With compound words, the plural suffix is normally added to the end of the word.
• cupfuls (not cupsful), ten-year-olds, mouse-traps

EXCEPTION: Some compound words add the plural suffix to that part which names the important person or object. (Consult your dictionary.)
• mothers-in-law (not mother-in-laws), pass-ersby (not passerbys), poets laureate (not poet laureates)

5.8 Third person singular verbs

5.8.1 Present tense third person singular verbs, which have the suffix -s, follow the rules for plurals above.
• look—looks, jump—jumps, push—pushes, marry—marries, sidestep—sidesteps, freeze-dry—freeze-dries

5.9 Possessives

5.9.1 Personal possessive pronouns do not use an apostrophe.
• his, hers, its, ours, yours, theirs

5.9.2 Most possessives of singular nouns, including proper names, or of indefinite pronouns, add -'s.
• somebody's mother, one dollar's worth
• boss's, man's, lady's, child's, boy's

EXCEPTION: Some proper names.
- always Jesus', Moses'
- sometimes Dickens', Richards', James', etc.

5.9.3   Possessives of plural nouns not ending in -s, add -'s.
- men's work, children's games

5.9.4   Possessives of plural nouns which end in -s, add only an apostrophe.
- two days' rest, five dollars' worth
- bosses', ladies', boys', Adamses'

5.9.5   Compound words and word groups add the possessive suffix (-'s or -') at the very end.
- commander in chief's, James and John's

EXCEPTION: To show separate ownership.
- James' and John's bodies collided.

6.   Prefix Rules

6.1   When a prefix is added, the spelling of the original word does not change.
- childlike, circumscribe, disagreeable

6.2   When a prefix ends with the same letter as the original word, do not drop one of the letters.
- illogical, misstep, unnatural, unnecessary

6.3   All words beginning with over- are spelled as one word, unhyphenated.
- overcast, overcharge, overhear

6.4   **Welcome** is one word with one **l**.

7.   Hyphen Rules

7.1   All words with the prefixes **all-, ex-, half-, quar-ter-, self-** are hyphenated.
• all-inclusive, ex-president, half-hearted, quar-ter-horse, self-control

7.2   Prefixes before proper names are always hy-phenated.
• pre-Christian, un-American

7.3   Prefixes are hyphenated to distinguish words spelled similarly.
• re-creation (vs. recreation), re-collect (vs. recollect), un-ionized (vs. unionized)

7.4   Prefixes are hyphenated to distinguish pronun-ciation of doubled vowels.
• re-enter, anti-inflammatory

7.5   Numbers from twenty-one to ninety-nine are hyphenated.
• twenty-one, ninety-nine

7.6   **Per cent** is never hyphenated.
• per cent, or percent, but never per-cent.

8. Capitalization Rules

8.1   Words are capitalized when they are specific names or titles of persons, places, or things (books, days, months).
• Moses, Judah, Jordan River, Bible, Sunday, January

8.2   Capitalized words retain their capitalization when they have a hyphenated prefix.
• pre-Christian, un-American

9. Contraction Rule

9.1   An apostrophe is placed where letters are removed.
• cannot—can't, are not—aren't, have not—haven't, we are—we're, we have—we've, that is—that's, let us—let's, of-the-clock—o'clock

10. Commonly Confused Spellings and Word Pairs

10.1   Confused spellings involving the word "all":

10.1.1   The word **all** has double l; but when combined with another syllable, it has single l.
• also, almost, already, altogether, withal

10.1.2   **All right** is always two words.
Alright is not recognized as standard English.

10.1.3   **Already** means *prior to some specified time.*
All ready means *completely ready.*
• By the time dinner was **all ready**, I was **already** hungry.

10.1.4   **Altogether** means *entirely.*
All together means *collectively.*
• There were **altogether** too many people **all together** in one room.

10.2   Confused spellings involving pronouns and contractions:

10.2.1   **Their** is the possessive of **they.**
They're is the contraction of **they are.**
There means *at that place.*
• **They're** moving **their** business over **there.**

10.2.2   **Your** is the possessive of **you.**
You're is the contraction of **you are.**
• **You're** leaving on **your** vacation.

10.2.3   **Whose** is the possessive of **who.**
Who's is the contraction of **who is.**
• **Whose** friend is it **who's** coming over?

10.2.4   **Its** is the possessive of **it.**
It's is the contraction of **it is.**
• **It's** my business to judge a book by **its** cover.

10.3   Confused word pairs

Anamixonyms are pairs of words which are easily confused because they are spelled similarly and/ or pronounced similarly, or they have similar meanings or usages. It is common to confuse the proper usage of the following select list of word pairs. With only a few exceptions, we have restricted this list to words of similar spelling or pronunciation. We have not included (1) words with identical pronunciations (*homophones*: bāse, bāss; see Section 17, Homophones), or (2) words with identical spellings but different pronunciations (*homographs*: bāss, băss), or (3) words with similar meanings or usages but dissimilar pronunciations or spellings (like, as; between, among).

10.3.1   Accede—*to give one's assent or agreement*
Exceed—*to go beyond, to surpass*
• I do not **accede** to your requests because they **exceed** the limits.

10.3.2   Accept—*to receive willingly*
Except—*to omit or to exclude*
• I **accept** all of your conditions **except** the last.

10.3.3   Access—*an entrance*
Excess—*a quantity beyond what is required*
• The manager has **access** to the **excess** funds.

10.3.4   Adapt—*to adjust to a situation*
Adept—*highly skilled or proficient*
Adopt—*to accept as one's own*
• John has **adopted** the goal of becoming **adept** at **adapting** to any situation.

10.3.5   Adverse—*opposed or hostile*
Averse—*reluctant, disinclined, uninterested*
• I am **averse** to climbing **adverse** terrain.

10.3.6 **Advice** (noun)—*opinion or counsel*
Advise (verb)—*to give advice or counsel*
• I **advise** you not to take his **advice**.

10.3.7 **Affect**—*to influence toward a change or to move the emotions*
Effect—*to produce or accomplish a result*
• The final **effect** of his plan **affected** everyone.

10.3.8 **Afflict**—*to cause great suffering or distress*
Inflict—*to deal a blow and give a wound*
• He has been **afflicted** for years from the blow **inflicted** upon him in his youth.

10.3.9 **Allot** (verb)—*to assign or distribute portions*
A lot (two words)—*very much*
Alot is not recognized as standard English.
• There is **a lot** of time to **allot** all portions.

10.3.10 **Allude** (allusion, allusive)—*to make an indirect reference without specifically identifying what is referred to*
Elude (elusion, elusive)—*to escape by cunning or deceit*
Illude (illusion, illusive)—*to deceive, to trick*
• His remarks **alluded** to the way in which he **eluded** capture by **illuding** his pursuers.

10.3.11 **Altar**—*an elevated place used in religious ceremonies*
Alter—*to adjust or modify without changing the fundamental nature*
• The carpenters came to the church in order to **alter** the structure of the **altar**.

10.3.12 **Assent** (verb)—*to express agreement*
Ascent (noun)—*an upward slope or incline*
• He gave his **assent** to climbing the rocky **ascent**.

10.3.13 Appraise—*to evaluate, to estimate the quality*
Apprise—*to inform, to cause to know*
- I apprise you of how to appraise antiques.

10.3.14 Assure—*to impart confidence or to remove doubt*
Ensure—*to guarantee, to make certain*
Insure—*to make safe or secure*
- I assure you that to insure the safety of the country will ensure your reelection.

10.3.15 Avoid—*to keep away from, to prevent from happening*
Evade—*to escape by cunning or deceit, to elude*
- While the police avoided the traffic jam, the suspect evaded capture.

10.3.16 Awhile (an adverb which is never preceded by a preposition)—*for a short time*
A while (two words which may be preceded by a preposition, such as for or in)—*a short time*
- Stay awhile. Stay for a while.
[*But not*: Stay for awhile.]

10.3.17 Bazaar—*a market or fair where miscellaneous articles are sold*
Bizarre—*strikingly unconventional*
- She sold a bizarre-looking coat at the club's annual bazaar.

10.3.18 Backward (adjective)—*facing toward the back, directed toward the past, done in reverse*
Backwards (adverb)—*to or toward the back, the rear, the past, in reverse*
- His backward policies have caused safety standards to slip backwards.

10.3.19 Beside (preposition)—*next to, at, by the side of*
Besides (adverb)—*in addition; also, moreover, furthermore*
- Besides me, there is nobody else beside you on the stage.

10.3.20 Capital—*the city which is the official seat of government*
Capitol—*the building where the legislature meets*
• We drove to the capital city, then walked up the capitol steps.

10.3.21 Censer—*a vessel in which to burn incense*
Censor (verb)—*to examine material and remove prohibited portions*, or (noun)—*someone who does this*
Censure—*an expression of disapproval*
Sensor—*a device which receives and responds to signals*
• The censor expressed his censure against placing a sensor in the censer.

10.3.22 Complement (verb)—*to complete, to make whole*, or (noun)—*something which completes*
Compliment (verb)—*to express praise, admiration, or congratulations*, or (noun)—*an expression of praise*
• I compliment the couple for how the talent of each complements the talent of the other.
• I gave him my compliments for supplying the amount – the complement which met our goal.

10.3.23 Continual—*frequently or regularly repeated*
Continuous—*unceasing, without interruption*
• The continual dripping of water finally led to a continuous stream of water.

10.3.24 Decent (adjective)—*honest and respectable*
Descent (noun)—*a decline*, or *a hereditary lineage*
Dissent (verb)—*to disagree*, or (noun)—*a disagreement*, or *the act of showing disagreement*
• The decent fellow traced his descent from those who expressed dissent.

10.3.25 Desert (noun)—*a wasteland*, or *that which is deserved*, or (verb)—*to forsake or abandon*
Dessert—*sweet food served at the end of a meal*

- The soldier **deserted** in the **desert,** and has received his just **deserts,** which included more than just no more **desserts** after meals.

10.3.26   Device (noun)—*an invention*
Devise (verb)—*to invent*
- She would **devise** a cleaning **device.**

10.3.27   Discreet—*showing prudence or judicious reserve*
Discrete—*constituting a separate thing, distinct*
- We must be **discreet** in how we perform each **discrete** step.

10.3.28   Disinterested—*not influenced by self-interest, impartial*
Uninterested—*not interested, indifferent*
- I was **uninterested** in your case until the **disinterested** witness defended you.

10.3.29   Elicit—*to draw out, to call forth, to evoke*
Illicit—*not allowed, illegal, unlawful*
- I tried to **elicit** a confession of his **illicit** drug traffic.

10.3.30   Emigrate—*to leave a country with plans to settle elsewhere*
Immigrate—*to enter and settle in a country from elsewhere*
- The Amish **emigrated** from Germany and im-**migrated** to America.

10.3.31   Eminent—*distinguished, outstanding in character or performance*
Immanent—*inherent, existing within*
Imminent—*impending, about to occur*
- The **eminent** theologian taught that God was **immanent** in the universe and that Christ's return was **imminent.**

10.3.32   Everyday (adjective)—*customary, routine, usual*
Every day (two words)—*each day consecutively*

- An **everyday** happening doesn't necessarily happen **every day**.

10.3.33   **Extant**—*still in existence, not lost or destroyed*
Extent—*the range over which something stretches*
- The **extant** manuscripts cover the full **extent** of ancient languages.

10.3.34   **Farther**—*more remote in physical distance*
Further—*more remote in anything except physical distance*
- The **farther** he traveled, the **further** his depression progressed.

10.3.35   **Faze** (verb)—*to interrupt the composure, to bother*
Phase (noun)—*one of a sequence of distinct forms of development*
- He's going through that **phase** where he tries to **faze** everyone with his questions.

10.3.36   **Imply**—*to suggest, to express indirectly*
Infer—*to deduce, to draw a conclusion from what is expressed*
- What the speaker **implied**, everyone else had already **inferred** from the facts.

10.3.37   **Lay** (laid, have laid, is laying, lays) (transitive verb)—*to place or put in a reclining position*
Lie (lay, have lain, is lying, lies) (intransitive verb)—*to be in or to place oneself in a reclining position*
Lie (lied, have lied, is lying, lies)—*to make a false statement*
- I **lay** the book down, and there it did **lie**.
- I **laid** the book down, and there it has **lain**.
- He **lied** when he said that he **laid** the book down and there it has **lain** for an hour.

10.3.38   **Personal** (adjective)—*pertaining to a particular individual or his private affairs*
Personnel (noun)—*the group of persons working in an organization*

- All of the personnel were allowed any time off to care for personal matters.

10.3.39 Principal (adjective)—*chief; the first, highest, or foremost in rank, importance, or worth*
Principle (noun)—*a basic truth, law, assumption, rule, or standard*
- The school principal stated that the principle of the rule of law is the principal foundation stone of our system of government.

10.3.40 Precede—*to come before in time, order, rank, or position*
Proceed—*to go forward, to continue an action*
- We will proceed without interruption until we reach that point which immediately precedes the end.

10.3.41 Raise (raised, have raised, is raising, raises) (transitive verb)—*to lift, to move, or to cause to move upward*
Rise (rose, have risen, is rising, rises) (intransitive verb)—*to ascend to a higher position*
- He rises out of bed, then raises the window.

10.3.42 Real (adjective)—*true, actual, genuine, authentic*
Really (adverb)—*truly, actually, genuinely, authentically*
- It was really helpful of you to give me the real facts.

10.3.43 Recent (noun)—*occurring at a time immediately prior to the present, modern, new*
Resent (verb)—*to feel indignantly grieved at someone or something*
- I resent your recent remarks.

10.3.44 Respectfully—*in a manner showing proper esteem or consideration*
Respectively—*in the order mentioned, each individually*
- I respectfully submit that John and Jane

respectively did not keep their parts of the agreement.

10.3.45 Set (set, have set, is setting, sets) (transitive verb)—*to place or to cause to be placed in a specified location or position*
Sit (sat, have sat, is sitting, sits) (intransitive verb)—*to be in a resting position*
- I set the book down, and there it sits.

10.3.46 Than (conjunction or preposition)—used in expressions of comparison
Then (adverb of order)—*at that time, in that order, in that case, in consequence, moreover*
- Then he concluded that he was more clever than you.

10.3.47 To (preposition)—*in a direction toward, or extending to a point of termination, until, up to*, or it introduces a verbal infinitive
Too (adverb)—*in addition, also, as well, very, indeed*
- There is too much to do to it and too little time to get to where we want to be.

10.3.48 Waiver—*the relinquishment of a right, a claim, or a privilege*
Waver—*to swing back and forth*, or *to hesitate or to show indecision*
- He wavers at signing the waiver.

Decoder

PHONICS RULES

11. Introduction

Many large books have been written about phonics, and many different methods have been used to teach phonics. In this booklet we are only attempting to list basic phonics rules in as few words as possible. There are exceptions to nearly every phonics rule. We have focused on the rules, not the exceptions.

The Decoder begins by listing general phonics rules. After this, it alphabetically lists various phonetic spellings. We have listed beside each letter of the alphabet all of its usual sounds and its significant combinations with other letters. Below this we have listed various phonetic rules involving this letter. At the end of the phonics rules is a phonics game.

12. Notation System

We have invented a special notation system to enable the reader to find quickly the information he is searching for in the Decoder. With a little practice, the Decoder will become very "handy."

12.1   Additional letters:
    ~ (tilde) indicates other letters *may* be (not *must* be) added to the syllable or word.

~ll~	could be llama, all, stallion, tortilla
~ti~	could be till, futile, nation, cities

12.2   Syllable divisions:
    ◇ (open diamond) indicates the beginning or the end of a syllable (which may also be the beginning or the end of a word).
    ◆ (black diamond) indicates the beginning or the end of a word.

◇a~	could be acorn, oasis, creative
◆a~	could be at, acorn, all
~e◇	could be fever, cedar, creative
~e◆	could be blue, tree, subtle

12.3   Consonants and vowels:
    ▣ (dotted square) indicates any consonant.
    ◉ (dotted circle) indicates any vowel.
    ◉̆ (dotted circle with breve) indicates a short vowel.
    ◉̄ (dotted circle with macron) indicates a long vowel.

~a▣◇	could be rap, rattle, always
~o◉~	could be oat, coat, hoe, oil
~◉̆~	could be ăt, bĕt, sĭt, cŏt, pŭt
~◉̄~	could be āte, cēdar, ī, hī, mōtor, flūte

12.4   Diacritical marks:
˘ (breve) marks short vowels.
‾ (macron) marks long vowels.
^ (circumflex) marks other vowel pronunciations.
¨ (diaeresis or umlaut) marks other vowel pronunciations.
˘ (caron) marks other consonant pronunciations.

ă, ĕ, ĭ, ŏ, ŭ, ў, ŏŏ	breve – short vowel sounds
ā, ē, ī, ō, ū, ȳ , ōō	macron – long vowel sounds
â, ê, î, ô, û, ŷ, ôô	circumflex – other vowel sounds, defined in context
ä, ë, ï, ö, ü, ÿ, öö	diaeresis – other vowel sounds, defined in context
č, ğ, ĭ, ǰ, ň, ř, š, ŭ, ž	caron – other consonant sounds, defined in context

13. Phonetic Syllable Division

In the Spelling Encoder we gave the dictionary rules for syllable division. These dictionary rules are used in the phonics rules on the following pages. You must recognize, however, that the dictionary division of words does not necessarily follow the actual way we divide words in natural speech. Observe the following:

ARTIFICIAL DICTIONARY DIVISION	ACTUAL PHONETIC DIVISION
act-or	ac-tor
an-i-mal	a-ni-mal
bat-ter	ba-tter
hab-it	ha-bit
help-er	hel-per
op-press	o-ppress
pol-i-cy	po-li-cy

Phonetic syllable division is simply the natural way we divide words as we speak. Here are the observable rules for how we break words as we pronounce them.

13.1   There is one phonetic syllable for each vowel sound ("ā" "ē" "ī" "ō" "ū" etc.), vowel blend sound ("ai" "oi" "au" "ou" etc.), or sometimes the semi-vowel sounds of "l" and "r."
- trou-ble = trou-b'l, trai-ler = trai-l'r

13.2   A phonetic syllable, whenever possible, begins with a consonant sound and ends with a vowel sound.
- sai-ling, pa-nel, se-ri-ous, mu-scle

13.3   A phonetic syllable will end with a semi-vowel sound,
- "f" "l" "m" "n" "r" "s" "th" "z" "w" "y"
or with a semi-vowel blend,
- "lf" "rf" "ls" "rs" "lth" "rth"
whenever the semi-vowel sound or blend is followed by another consonant sound,
- sal-ty, pan-da, ser-vant, serf-dom, pars-ly, earth-ly
unless the consonants form a combination, in which case the blend goes with the next syllable.
- mu-stard, a-flame, e-sta-blish

The Phonetic Decoder uses the dictionary rules for syllable division, not these natural rules. It is easy to confuse the two, so be aware.

14. General Phonics Rules

14.1 Vowels a, e, o, u, at the end of a syllable, are usually long, except at the end of a word.

~ā◇	ācorn, volcāno, āorta
~ē◇	ēmit, cēdar, ēon
~ō◇	stōry, mōbile, lōcate
~ū◇	ūniform, hūmor, būgle

14.2 When there is a single consonant between two vowels, the first vowel is almost always long.

~◌̃ ◻◉~	māle, pūpil, nōtāte

14.3 When there are two consonants between two vowels, the first vowel is almost always short.

~◌̃ ◻◻◉~	ŭntil, ălley, tăcker

14.4 When there is one vowel in the middle of a one syllable word, that vowel is usually short.

◆◻◌̃ ◻◆	păt, pĕt, pĭt, pŏt, rŭb

14.5 The vowels i and o may be long if followed by two consonants, especially nd and ld.

~ī◻◻~	bīnd, fīnd, mīnd, mīld, wīnd, wīld
~ō◻◻~	ōld, bōld, cōld, fōld, bōlt, cōlt, jōlt

14.6 Primitive words do not end with a long ā, but with a long āy (except the article "a").

~ay◆	prāy, hāy, dāy

14.7a c before e, i, or y always says "s."

14.7b c not before e, i, or y says hard "k."

~ce~	cent, face, dancer
~ci~	city, cider, pencil,
~cy~	cypress, cyclone, policy
~c~	cat, claw, crown, cone

14.8a g before e, i, or y usually says "j."

EXCEPTION:
- get, girl, give

14.8b g not before e, i, or y says hard "g."

~ge~	gesture, genes, cage
~gi~	giraffe, gist, logical
~gy~	gym, gypsy, apology
~g~	glass, go, gall

14.9 ei says the long "ā" sound, unless it follows c, when it says long "ē." (See also 15.9.8-11.)

| ~êi~ | êight, hêir, rêign, bêige, hêinous |
| ~cêi~ | decêit, recêipt, recêive |

14.10 ie says the long "ē" sound, except at the end of a primitive one-syllable word, when it may say the long "ī" sound. (See also 15.5.12-13.)

| ~iē~ | priest, brownie, collie, prairie |
| ◆~īe◆ | die, lie, pie, tie |

14.11 The past tense ending -ed says "d" or "t" and does not form a separate syllable.

| ~ed◆ | lived (liv'd), jumped (jump't) |

EXCEPTION: When the simple verb ends with d or t, -ed forms a separate syllable which says "ed."

| ~ded◆ | sided |
| ~ted◆ | parted |

14.12　The "sh" sound is spelled sh at the beginning or end of a primitive word.

| ◆sh~ | shock |
| ~sh◆ | hush |

EXCEPTION:
• sugar, schiller

14.13　Within a word, the "sh" sound is spelled ci, sci, si, ssi, ti, s(ū), or ss(ū).

~ci~ , ~sci~	special, conscience
~si~ , ~ssi~	tension, passion
~ti~	nation
~sū~ , ~ssū~	censure, tissue

EXCEPTION:
• the suffix -ship

| ~ship~ | worshiper, kinship, battleship |

14.14　si and su (not ti or ci) can also say "zh."

| ~si~ | vision, fusion, adhesion |
| ~su~ | measure, pleasure |

14.15　r changes the sound of short vowels before it:
　　　　r swallows up the sound of short e, i, or u;
　　　　r alters the short "ă" sound to broad "ä" sound;
　　　　r alters the short "ŏ" sound to long "ō" sound.

~ĕr~	person (p'r-son), herd (h'rd)
~ĭr~	stir (st'r), fir (f'r)
~ŭr~	purchase (p'r-chase), curse (c'rse)
~är~	fär, lärge, scärlet
~ōr~	cōrn, stōrm, fōrtify

15. Alphabetic Phonics Rules

The following pages go through the alphabet, letter by letter, and explain how to read the letter code. Under each letter we have listed:

SOUNDS:
  The usual sounds represented by this letter.

DIPHTHONGS:
  Vowels (including w and y) which may join with this letter (if it is a vowel) to represent a blended vowel sound.

COMBINATIONS:
  Vowels (including g, h, w, and y) which may combine with this letter (if it is a vowel) to "spell" or represent one vowel sound.

OPENERS:
  Letters (including vowels) which may combine or blend with this letter to represent a consonant sound or sounds at the beginning of a syllable.

CLOSERS:
  Letters which may combine or blend with this letter to represent a consonant sound or sounds at the end of a syllable.

Special notations:
        [ ] (brackets) around a letter in a spelling means the letter is silent in the combination.
        ( ) (parentheses) around a letter in a spelling means the letter is an optional addition to the combination.
        / (forward slash) means "or."

These listings are almost exhaustive. (We have omitted some of the rare, one-of-a-kind, and foreign spellings, such as bdellium, yacht, angst.)

After these listings, we have given specific spellings and rules for decoding them.

A

SOUNDS:
ācre, ăt, wäll

DIPHTHONGS:
wāit, hāy, aisle, aye, häul, äwe

COMBINATIONS:
aa, ae, ag, ah, ai, aigh, au, augh, ay, ea, eau, oa

OPENERS:
ia, ua, wa, wea, wha, whea, ya, yea

15.1

15.1.1 a is long in a syllable which ends in a.

| ~ā◇ | ācorn, bācon, volcāno
(but fäther) |

15.1.2 a is short in a syllable which ends in a consonant.

| ~ă~▣ | ăm, ănd, rănch, ăpple, trănsfer,
diaphrăgm
(but äll, yächt) |

15.1.3 a is broad when it ends a word.

| ~ä♦ | umbrellä, cobrä, formulä
(but bologna) |

15.1.4 a is long when followed by a consonant and silent e.

| ~ā▣e~ | āle, tāke, dāre, brācelet |

15.1.5 In foreign spellings, a is usually broad.

| ~ä~ | moräle, miräge, locäle |

15.1.6 ae is a Latin spelling for long ē or short ĕ.

| ~aē~
~aĕ~ | Caēsar, paēon, algaē
aĕsthetic
(but mäelstrom) |

15.1.7   **ah** always says the broad "ä" sound.

~äh~	äh, hurräh, bäh, shäh, sähib

15.1.8   **ai** almost always says the long "ā" sound.

~āi~	āil, stāir, brāise
	(but plaid, said, mountain, aīsle)

15.1.9   **al** at the end of a polysyllabic word is almost always reduced to a semi-syllable ('l). At the end of a one-syllable word, **al** has short ă.

◇~al♦	royal (roy'l), principal (princip'l)
♦~ăl♦	Ăl, găl, Hăl, păl

15.1.10   **al** followed by a vowel (except silent e) in a stressed syllable almost always has short ă.

~ăl◇◉~	sălary, vălue, fatălity, pălace

15.1.11   **al** followed by a consonant in the same syllable has broad ä, silent l.

~äl▣◇~	äll, cälm, älms, psälms, tälk, sält
	(but călf, hälf)

15.1.12   **al** followed by a consonant in a different syllable usually has broad ä.

~äl◇▣~	älmost, fälter, älmond

15.1.13   **al** followed by a consonant in a different syllable sometimes has short ă.

~ăl◇▣~	ălley, găllop, ălbum, călcium,
	mălfunction

15.1.14   **a** followed by **nge** almost always has long ā.

~änge~	stränge, mänger, gränge
	(but änger, tängerine)

15.1.15   A single r at the end of a word, or followed by a consonant within a syllable, or followed by a consonant in the next syllable, makes what would have been the short "ä" sound into the broad "ä" sound.

~är♦	fär, jär
~är▣~◇	lärk, lärge
~är◇▣~	scärlet, härvest

15.1.16   An a followed by either a double r, or by an r followed by a vowel, phonetically carries the "r" sound over to the next syllable, and the a becomes a long ā.

~ārr~	mārry, cārrot, gārrison
~ār◉~	tāriff, chārity

15.1.17   a followed by ste is almost always long ā.

~āste~	tāste, wāste, chāsten (but fǎsten)

15.1.18   Vowel blend äu usually represents broad ä.

~äu~	säucer, häunted, appläuse
~äugh~	cäught, häughty, täught (but lǎugh, gāuge, mauve, dinosaur, sauerkraut, restaurant)

15.1.19   Vowel blend äw always represents broad ä.

~äw~	äwe, päw, yäwn, äwkward

15.1.20   Vowel blend ay often represents long ā.

~āy~	clāy, māyor, portrāy, pāyable (but says, quay, aye, bayou)

B

15.2

SOUNDS:
bubble
OPENERS:
bl, br
CLOSERS:
[b]t(s), bs, lb(s), m[b](s), rb(s)

15.2.1 Single consonant b

| ~b~ | bob, curb, bulb, oboe |

15.2.2 Double consonant b

| ~bb~ | babble, bubble, rubber, |

15.2.3 Consonant blend bl

| ~bl~ | black, bleak, blind, blow, blue, sublime |

15.2.4 Consonant blend br

| ~br~ | brake, break, brick, broke, brut, celebrate |

15.2.5 b is silent before t or after m when they are in the same syllable.

| ~bt~ | doubt, debt (also in two syllables: subtle, but subtitle) |
| ~mb~ | crumb, dumb, thumbnail |

C

15.3

SOUNDS:
city, corn, očean, child, chrome, čhef
OPENERS:
ci, cl, cr, ch(l/r), [c]z, [s]c, sch(l/m/n/r/w)
CLOSERS:
ch(s), ck(s), (l/r)cs, [c]t(s), lc, nc(k)(s), rc(s), sc(s)

15.3.1a When c is not followed by e, i, or y, it usually has the hard "k" sound.

| ~c~ | act, coast, creed, objection, attic |

15.3.1b When c is followed by e, i, or y, it usually has the soft "s" sound.

~ce~	cent, face, exceed (but cello)
~ci~	city, pencil, society
~cy~	cyclone, cypress, policy

15.3.2 When c is followed by e or i and another vowel (especially a or o), it often has the soft "sh" sound.

| ~čeʘ~ | očean, herbačeous |
| ~čiʘ~ | sočial, deličious |

15.3.3 When c is doubled, the first c has the hard "k" sound and the second c is silent, unless followed by e or i, when it is pronounced as "s."

~cc~	acclaim, accompany, occult
~cce~	accent, accept
~cci~	accident, occidental

15.3.4 Consonant blend cl

| ~cl~ | cluck, class, declaration, uncle |

15.3.5 Consonant blend cr

| ~cr~ | crew, cradle, secretary, lucre |

15.3.6 ch often has the dental sound of "tsh."

| ~ch~ | child, church, wrench, merchant |

15.3.7 ch has the "k" sound in the English spelling of the Greek letter "chi."

| ~ch~ | chorus, chrome, echo, stomach |

15.3.8 ch has the "sh" sound in French words.

~čh~	čhandelier, mustačhe, mačhine

15.3.9 ck and cqu always have the "k" sound.

~ck~	kicker, wreck, hickory
~cqu~	lacquer

15.3.10 cz may have the soft "ch" sound.

~cz~	Czech, czardas

15.3.11 c is silent before another consonant when it would be phonetically harsh to pronounce it.

~c▢~	muscle, indictment, drachm, Czar

15.3.12 sc blends to make the "s" sound when it is followed by e or i in the same syllable.

◇sci~◇	science, ascension
	(but conscience)

D

SOUNDS:
daddy

OPENERS:
dr, dw

15.4

CLOSERS:
dg, ds, dz, ld(s), nd(s), rd(s)

15.4.1 Single consonant d

~d~	did, blind, made

15.4.2 Double consonant d

~dd~	daddy, huddle, forbidden

15.4.3 Consonant blend dr

~dr~	drink, dresser, drop

15.4.4 Consonant blend dw

~dw~	dwell, dwarf, dwindle

15.4.5 Consonant-vowel blend **di** says the "ji" sound.

~di~	soldier

15.4.6a **dge** says the "j" sound. The final **e** makes the **g** soft; the letter **d** inserts a consonant, which makes the preceding vowel short.

~ŏ̇ dge~	fŭdge, brĭdge, bădger

15.4.6b American spelling sometimes drops the silent **e** when adding a suffix.

~ŏ̇ dg◇▫~	jŭdgment, flĕdgling, abrĭdgment

15.4.7 **dj** says the "j" sound.

~dj~	adjourn, adjust, adjective

15.4.8 Consonant-vowel blend **du** say the "ju" sound.

~du~	educate, schedule, gradual

15.4.9 **d** blends into silence when it would be phonetically harsh to pronounce it between **n** and another consonant.

~nd~	handkerchief, handsome

E

15.5

SOUNDS:
  hē, ĕxit, cafê
DIPHTHONGS:
  veil, hey, surfeit, eye, die, feud, few
COMBINATIONS:
  ae, ea, eau, ee, eg, eh, ei, eig, eigh, eo, eou, ey, ie, oe, ue
OPENERS:
  ie, ue, we, wea, whe, whea, ye, yea

15.5.1 **e** is long when it ends a syllable.

~ē◇   hē, idēa, cēdar

15.5.2   e is short in a syllable which ends in a conso-
          nant.

~ĕ▢◇   ĕxit, bĕll, forgĕt

15.5.3a   e at the end of a word is silent when it is pre-
          ceded by a vowel and a consonant.

~ŏ̄ ▢e♦   pirate, native, purpose

15.5.3b   If the last syllable is stressed, the preceding
          vowel is usually long.

~ŏ̄ ▢e♦   debāte, derīve, suppōse

15.5.4a   e is silent when it is at the end of a word and is
          preceded by a vowel and two consonants. The
          preceding vowel is almost always short.

~ŏ̄ ▢▢e♦   lărge, sĕrve, syrĭnge, brŏnze, cŭrve

15.5.4b   When the two consonants before the e are
          identical, the word is of French origin, and the
          last syllable is almost always stressed.

~ŏ̄ ▢▢e♦   crevasse, rosette, chenille

15.5.5   When two e's are separated by one consonant,
          the first e is almost always long and the second
          e is almost always silent.

~ē▢e~   ēvening, mērely, extrēmely
                       (but ēven)

15.5.6   In words of Greek origin, final e or es is always
          long.

~ē♦   acmē, apostrophē, hyperbolē
~ēs♦   diabetēs, appendicēs, indicēs

15.5.7 In words of French origin, final e, ee, or et often has the long "ā" sound. (There are many exceptions here.)

~ê♦	cafê, clichê, sautê
~êe♦	entrêe, matinêe, negligêe
~êt♦	valêt, bouquêt, crochêt

15.5.8 ea can represent the long or the short sound of e, or occasionally the long "ā" sound.

~ēa~	mēan, hēave, brēathe
~ĕa~	mĕant, hĕavy, brĕath
	(but brêak, stêak, grêat)

15.5.9 r always swallows up the short "ĕ" sound of ea. (Don't confuse this with the long "ē" sound in "fēar" or the long "ā" sound in "bêar.")

~ĕar~	earnest ('r-nest), learn (l'rn), yearn (y'rn), certain (c'r-tain)
	(but heart)

15.5.10a The past tense ending, -ed, is pronounced "ĕd" whenever it follows d or t.

~ĕd♦	decided, branded, belated, wasted

15.5.10b e is silent and only d is pronounced after a voiced consonant (b, g, j, l, m, n, r, v, w, y, z).

~ed♦	sobbed (sobb'd), dodged (dodg'd), called (call'd), damned (damn'd), barred (barr'd), saved (sav'd), bowed (bow'd), bayed (bay'd), buzzed (buzz'd)

15.5.10c e is silent and d is pronounced as "t" after an unvoiced consonant (f, k, p, s, x).

~ed♦	puffed (puff't), baked (bak't), topped (topp't), boxed (box't), guessed (guess't)

15.5.11   Double e regularly says the long "ē" sound. (But see 15.5.7.)

~ēe~	fēe, dēed, discrēet
	(but been)

15.5.12   ei commonly says the long "ā" sound, unless it follows c, when it says the long "ē" sound. (See also 14.10.)

~êi~	hêir, hêinous, rêindeer
	(but heifer, forfeit, seismic)
~cēi~	decēit, recēive, recēipt

15.5.13   eig and eigh usually say the long "ā" sound.

~êig~	rêign, invêigle, bêige
	(but foreign, sovereign)
~êigh~	êight, nêighbor, wêigh
	(but height)

15.5.14a   When eo represents one vowel sound at the end of a syllable, it may have either long "ē," short "ĕ," or long "ō" sound. (See also 15.7.4-5.)

~ēo◇	pēople
~ĕo◇	jĕopardy, lĕopard
~eō◇	yeōman

15.5.14b   When eo divides between two syllables, e is always long, but o is usually short, except when o ends the word.

~ē◇ŏ~	gēŏgraphy, nēŏn, pēŏn
	(but dēōderant)
~ē◇ō♦	orēō, rodēō, sterēō, vidēō

15.5.15   r always swallows up the short "ĕ" sound.

~er~	fisher (fish'r), person (p'rson),
	merge (m'rge), certain (c'rtain)

15.5.16   Doubled r lengthens the short "ĕ" sound toward
           the "ê" (long "ā") sound.

~êrr~	bĕrry, ĕrror, tĕrrible

15.5.17   The plural ending -es (pronounced "ĕz") is used
           with words ending with the sounds of "s" (soft
           č), "z," "sh" (soft ch), "tch" (hard ch), "j" (soft g),
           "zh," "x" (cks). (Compare 15.5.6.)

~ĕs♦	facĕs, blazĕs, fishĕs, finchĕs, cagĕs, orangĕs, duchessĕs, fixĕs

15.5.18   eu and ew always say the long "ū" (long ōō or
           yōō) sound.

~eû~	sleûth, deûce, neûtral eûlogy, feûd, therapeûtic
~eŵ~	bleŵ, streŵn, leŵd, seŵer eŵe, feŵ, heŵn, jeŵelry (but sew)

15.5.19   ey commonly says the long "ē" sound, usually in
           unstressed syllables.

~ēy~	kēy, monēy, jockēy, abbēy (but eye)

15.5.20   ey in some primary words has the long "ā"
           sound, usually in stressed syllables.

~êy~	hêy, convêy, survêyor

F

SOUNDS:
  fluffy
OPENERS:
  fl, fr

15.6   CLOSERS:
             fs, ft(s), lf(s), rf(s)

15.6.1   Single consonant f

~f~	far, prefer, fifty
	(but of, where f says the "v" sound)

15.6.2　f is often doubled after a short vowel, especially at the end of a word.

~ŏ ff~	flŭff, dïfficult, mastïff
	(but if, of, chef, clef)

15.6.3　Consonant blend fl

~fl~	fling, flat, inflation
~ffl~	baffle, raffle, affluent

15.6.4　Consonant blend fr

~fr~	frog, freezing, confronted

G

SOUNDS:
gaggle, ğeneral, garağe
COMBINATIONS:
ag, aig, augh, eg, eig, eigh, ig, igh, ough, ug, ugh
OPENERS:
g[h], gi, gl, [g]n gr, gu
CLOSERS:
(r)gh(s), gm, gn, gs, dg, lg(s), ng(s), rg(s)

15.7

15.7.1a　Single g often has the hard "g" sound, unless it is followed by the vowels e, i, or y.

~g~	gag, triangle, lagoon, goulash

15.7.1b　When a single g is followed by the vowels e, i, or y, it commonly has the "j" sound.

~ğe~	ğem, ğentle, cağe, rangě, progěny (but gear, geese)
~ği~	ğiant, region, strategic, longitude (but girl, give)
~ğy~	strateğy, bioloğy, ğypsy (but gynecology)

15.7.2 Double g has the hard "g" sound.

| ~gg~ | egg, shaggy, ragged
(but exaggerate) |

15.7.3 In French words, g says the "zh" sound.

| ~ğe~ | rouğe, beiğe, garağe, bourğeoisie |

15.7.4 -geon and -gion are pronounced "jun."

| ~geon | surgeon, pigeon |
| ~gion | contagion, religion |

15.7.5 -geous and -gious are pronounced "jus."

| ~geous | gorgeous |
| ~gious | religious |

15.7.6 gh is often silent when it follows a vowel in the same syllable.

| ◇~◉gh~◇ | straight, through, weight |

15.7.7 gh says the hard "g" sound when it precedes a vowel in the same syllable.

| ◇gh◉~◇ | ghost, aghast, sorghum |

15.7.8 gh at the end of a primitive word sometimes has the "f" sound.

| ~gh♦ | cough, laugh, enough |

15.7.9 Consonant blend gl with hard "g" sound

| ~gl~ | glitter, gloomy, glad, bugle, juggle |

15.7.10 When g is followed by m or n in the same syllable, the g is silent.

| ◇~gm~◇ | diaphragm, phlegm, paradigm (contrast frag-ment) |
| ◇~gn~◇ | gnat, poignant, sign, reign, impugn (contrast preg-nant) |

15.7.11 Consonant blend gr with hard "g" sound

| ~gr~ | green, great, bluegrass |

15.7.12 When u is inserted between g and e or between g and i, it prevents the g from saying the soft "j" sound.

| ~gue~ | vogue, guess, guernsey |
| ~gui~ | penguin, guild, guile |

(See also ng, ough.)

H

15.8

SOUNDS:
  hair, heir
COMBINATIONS:
  ah, aigh, augh, eh, igh, ih, oh, ooh, ough, ugh, uh
OPENERS:
  ch(l/r), gh, ph(l/r), rh, sch(l/m/n/r/w), sh(r), th(r), wh, zh
CLOSERS:
  ch(s), gh(s), ph(s), rh, (r)sh, th(s), wha, whe, whea, whi, who

15.8.1 Consonant h

| ~◇h◉~ | house, cohort, horse |

15.8.2 h is silent in words borrowed from French.

| ~◇h◉~ | hour, honest, graham |

15.8.3   h is not pronounced when it follows a vowel in the same syllable.

~◉h◇   ah, ahah, hurrah, eh, nihilism, oh, ohm, John, uh

15.8.4   h is not pronounced when its pronunciation would be phonetically difficult – usually when it begins a syllable immediately after a syllable ending with a consonant.

~▣◇h~   exhibit, shepherd

(See also ch, gh, ph, rh, sh, th, wh.)

I

15.9

SOUNDS:
   īvy, ĭf, skî,
   savĭor (consonantal y" sound)
DIPHTHONGS:
   wāit, aisle, veil, surfeit, die, oil
COMBINATIONS:
   ai, aigh, ei, eig, eigh, ie, ig, igh, ih, io, oi, ui, uoi(s)
OPENERS:
   ci, gi, ia, ie, io, si, ti, ui, whi, wi, zi

15.9.1   i is usually long when it ends a syllable.

~ī◇   Ī, tīger, bīson, reprīsal

15.9.2   i at the end of a word may make the long "ī" or the long "ē" sound.

~ī♦   alkalī, alibī, alumnī
~î♦   skî, yogî, chilî, taxî

15.9.3   i is commonly short in a syllable which ends in a consonant.

~ĭ~▣◇   ĭn, strĭng, relĭgion, dĭgger

15.9.4a   If i is followed by another vowel, the following
           vowel is often part of another syllable, and a
           consonantal "y" sound appears between the two
           vowels.

15.9.4b   In a primitive word or a stressed syllable, when
           i is followed by a vowel beginning another syl-
           lable, the i says the long "ī" sound.

~ī◇◉~	dīal (dī-y'l), dīet (dī-y't), vīolet (vī-yo-l't), iambic (ī-yam-bic)

15.9.4c   In a suffix or an unstressed syllable, when i is
           followed by a vowel beginning another syllable,
           the i says the long "ē" sound.

~î◇◉~	librarîan (li-bra-rî-y'n), copîer (cop-î-y'r), curîous (cur-î-yous), aquarîum (a-qua-rî-yum)

15.9.5   When i begins a syllable, the i is swallowed up
           by the consonantal "y" sound.

◇ĭ◉~	brillĭant (brill-yant), spanĭel (span-yel), companĭon (com-pan-yon), savĭor (sav-yor)

15.9.6   Many foreign words give i a long "ē" sound.

~i~	magazîne, debrîs, intrîgue

15.9.7   When followed by a consonant and a silent e, i
           is commonly long in stressed syllables and short
           in unstressed syllables.

~ī▫e~	līke, fīre, decīde, retīre
~ĭ▫e~	motĭve, hypocrĭte, medicĭne

15.9.8   At the end of a primitive word, ie says the long
           "ī" sound.

~īe◆	līe, untīe, magpīe

15.9.9   As a suffix, ie says the long "ē" sound.

~îe♦	prairîe, eerîe collîe

15.9.10   Within a primitive word, ie says the long "ē" sound.

~îe~	prîest, shrîek, besîege, fîend,
~îeld~	yîeld, fîelder
~îef~	chîef, grîef, belîef,
~îeve~	achîeve, grîeve, belîeve
~îer~	pîerce, frontîer, tîer
	(but sieve, friend, conscience)

15.9.11   When adding the past tense ending d, or the plural (sometimes present tense) ending s, to words ending in ie (or y changed to ie), the ie sounds the same as in the original word.

~īed♦	dry—drīed—drīes (long "ī" sound)
~īes♦	dignify—dignifīed—dignifīes
~îed♦	candy—candîed—candîes (long "ē"
~îes♦	sound)
	vary—varîed—varîes

15.9.12   igh always says the long "ī" sound.

~īgh~	hīgh, līght, rīghteous

15.9.13a   When i is followed by gn, ld, or nd in the same syllable, then the i is long.

~īgn◇~	sīgn, malīgn
~īld◇~	wīld, chīld
~īnd◇~	kīnd, behīnd

15.9.13b   When the consonant combinations gn, ld, or nd are divided between syllables, the preceding i is often short.

~ĭg◇n~	sĭgnal, malĭgnant
~ĭl◇d~	wĭlderness, chĭldren
~ĭn◇d~	kĭndred, hĭndrance

15.9.14   When ir, or ir plus another consonant, occurs at the end of a syllable, the r swallows up the short "ĭ" sound.

~ir◇	fir (f'r), stir (st'r), dirt (d'rt)
~ir▣~◇	birth (b'rth), affirm (aff'rm)

15.9.15   In a primitive word, when ir is followed by a vowel or by another r (not when adding a suffix, as in tiring, stirring), the i usually says the long "ē" sound.

~îr◇◉~	mîracle (like mere), spîrit (like spear)
~îr◇r◉~	mîrror, îrritate, stîrrup

(See also ci, si, ti.)

J

SOUNDS:
  jelly

15.10

15.10.1   Consonant j

~j~	jelly, object, adjective, rejoice

15.10.2   In some foreign words, j has an "h" sound, a consonantal "y" sound, or a "zh" sound.

~j~	Spanish: jalapeno (halapeno)
	Latin (from Hebrew): hallelujah (-yah)
	French: jabot (zhăbō)

K

SOUNDS:
kicker

OPENERS:
kl, [k]n, kr, sk

15.11

CLOSERS:
ks, ck(s), lk(s), nk(s), rk(s), sk(s)

15.11.1   Consonant k

~k~	king, skillful, crinkle

15.11.2   k is silent before n only at the beginning of a primitive word.

◆kn~	know, knot, knead, knife

(See also ck.)

L

SOUNDS:
lull

OPENERS:
bl, cl, chl, fl, gl, kl, pl, phl, sl

15.12

CLOSERS:
lb(s), lc, ld(s), lf(s), lg, lk(s), [l]m(s), [l]n(s), lp(s), ls, lt(s), ltz, lv(es), lz, rl(s), sle(s)

15.12.1   Single consonant l

~l~	look, sleep, politics

15.12.2   When l is pronounced after a long vowel – especially after long ī or long ū – a consonantal "y" or "w" sound often appears, creating a semi-syllable (y'l, w'l).

◇~ŏl~◇	male (mā-y'l), meal (mē-y'l), mile (mī-y'l), mole (mō-w'l), mule (mū-w'l)

15.12.3   When l is doubled, the preceding vowel is short.

~ŏll~	bĕll, dwĕll, windmĭll

15.12.4   When a consonant plus l occurs after a vowel, and before an e, and if the first of the two syllables is stressed, then the first vowel may be long (contrary to general phonics rule 14.3).

~o͞ ◇▣le	āble, tītle, nōble, rūble

15.12.5   When two consonants plus the letter l occur between two vowels, then the first vowel is short.

~o͝ ▣▣le~	ăpple, kĕttle, tĭckle, bŏttle, pŭddle

15.12.6a   When letter l is preceded by a or o, and is followed by k or m, the letter l is usually not pronounced, and the vowels are pronounced as broad "ä" or long "ō."

~◇älk◇~	tälk, chälk
~◇ōlk◇~	fōlk, yōlk
~◇älm◇~	pälm, psälm
~◇ōlm◇~	Hōlmes

15.12.6b   When letter l is preceded by a or o, and is followed by f or v, the letter l is usually not pronounced, and the vowels are pronounced as short "ă" or short "ŏ."

~◇älf◇~	cälf, hälf
~◇ŏlf◇~	gŏlf (but wolf)
~◇älv◇~	cälve, hälve, sälve
~◇ŏlv◇~	sŏlve, invŏlve (but wolves)

15.12.7   In some foreign words, ll has the consonantal "y" sound.

~ll~	tortilla (tōr-tî-yä)

M

SOUNDS:
mommy
OPENERS:
sm, [m]n
15.13
CLOSERS:
[l]m(s), m[b](s), m[n](s), mp(s),
m[p]t(s), ms, rm(s), sm(s)

15.13.1   Single consonant m

~m~	mist, clamp, sum

15.13.2   Double consonant m

~mm~	mommy, hammock, summer

15.13.3a   When m is followed by b, n, or p in the same syllable, the b, n, or p is silent.

~mb◇~	crumb, thumb
~mn◇~	autumn, solemn, hymn
~mp◇~	redemption, exemption

15.13.3b   When m is followed by b, n, or p in a separate syllable, the b, n, or p is pronounced.

~m◇b~	crumble, thimble
~m◇n~	autumnal, solemnify, hymnal
~m◇p~	exemplify

15.13.4   When mn begins a word, m is silent.

◆mn~	mnemonic

15.13.5   When sm ends a word, s is voiced ("z" sound) and a semi-syllable appears (z'm).

~sm◆	prism (pri-z'm), chasm (cha-z'm), spasm (spa-z'm)

N

SOUNDS:
nanny

OPENERS:
sn, [g]n, [k]n, [m]n, [p]n

CLOSERS:
[l]n(s), [m]n(s), nc(s), nd(s), ng(s),
nk(s), ns, nt(s), nx, nz, rn(s)

15.14.1   Single consonant n

| ~n~ | nine, noon, stand |

15.14.2   Double consonant n

| ~nn~ | nanny, banner, inner |

15.14.3   When a primitive word ends in an unstressed vowel plus n, the n often swallows up the vowel sound, reducing it to a semi-syllable.

| ~⊙n♦ | artisan (ar-ti-z'n), citizen (ci-ti-z'n) |
| | basin (ba-s'n), beacon (bea-c'n) |

15.14.4   An ng at the end of a primitive word or suffix blends into a nasal-palatal "ng" sound.

| ~ng~♦ | sing, sang, sung, song, angst |

15.14.5   When n and g are in separate syllables, n has the "ng" sound, and g has the hard "g" sound.

| ~n◇g~ | longer, anger, finger, ingot |

15.14.6   When ng is followed by e, then g has the "j" sound, except before the suffix -er.

| ~nge◇ | binge, hinge, tangent |
| ~nger~ | longer, anger, finger |

15.14.7   When n is followed by a "k" sound, such as hard c, k, q, or x (ks), then the "ng" sound is followed by the "k" or "ks" sound.

~nc~	zinc, sanction
~nk~	blink, blanket
~nq~	propinquity
~nx~	lynx, anxious

(See also **gn, kn.**)

O

15.15

SOUNDS:
nō, ŏn, cöme,
tōō (long "ōō" sound = lûcid),
tŏŏk (short "ŏŏ" sound = püt)

DIPHTHONGS:
ōil, bōy, ŏut, ŏwl, ōwe

COMBINATIONS:
eo, eou, io, oa, oe, oh, oi, oo, ooh,
ou, ough, uois, uoy

OPENERS:
io, uo, uoi, who, wo, yo, you

15.15.1   o is long in a syllable which ends in o.

~ō◇~	nō, stōry, mōbile

15.15.2   o is short in a syllable which ends in a consonant. (Short "ŏ" sound = the broad "ä" sound.)

~ŏ▫◇~	ŏn, hŏt, fŏx, chrŏnic, ŏften, ŏbject

15.15.3   o is short before two consonants in the same syllable.

~ŏ▫▫◇~	ŏff, clŏth, respŏnd

15.15.4   o may have the short "ŭ" sound, as in "pŭtt," where you might expect a long or short "o" sound.

~ö~	cöme, wön, cömfort, gövernment

15.15.5   When **oa** is in one syllable, it says long "ō."

~ōa~	gōat, rōad, bōard

15.15.6 When oe ends a primitive word, it almost always says long "ō."

~ōe◆	dōe, fōe, hōe, rōebuck, tōe, wōe

15.15.7 When oi is in one syllable, it is a vowel blend for the "oy" sound.

~oi~	foil, noise, pointer

15.15.8 oo has the long "ōō" sound of "too" when it ends a syllable, or when it is followed by f, h, l, m, n, p, s, th, v, or z.

~ōō◇	bōō, dōōdle, mōō, pōōdle, tōō, vōōdōō
	prōōf, pōōh, fōōl, brōōm, nōōn, lōōp,
~ōō▣~	lōōse, tōōth, grōōve, snōōze

15.15.9 oo has the short "ŏŏ" sound of "took" when it is followed by k.

~ŏŏk~	tŏŏk, crŏŏked, brŏŏk

15.15.10 oo has the long "ō" sound of "door" when it is followed by r.

~oor~	flōor, dōor, mōor, pōor

15.15.11 oo, when followed by d may have any of the three vowel sounds of the letter u, and when followed by t may have two of the three sounds.

	the "û" or long "ōō" sound:
~ōōd~	food, mood, moot, boot, shoot
	the "ü" or short "ŏŏ" sound:
~ŏŏt~	good, wood, hood, foot, soot
	the short "ŭ" sound:
~ood~	blood, flood, root, soot

15.15.12 When or occurs within a syllable, the r makes the o long where it might not be otherwise.

◇~ōr~◇　　　ōr, cōrn, stōrm, fōrtify

15.15.13a When orr is followed by a short vowel sound, the o is long.

~ōrrŏ~　　　hōrrĭble, tōrrĕnt, cōrrĕct, pōrrĭdge

15.15.13b When orr is followed by a long vowel sound, it phonetically carries the "r" sound off with the next syllable, and the o becomes a short ŏ. (The word horror is an exception, because the second or overpowers the first orr).

~ŏrrō~　　　sŏrry, bŏrrōw, tomŏrrōw, cŏrrōde

15.15.14 When o is followed by one consonant and silent e, the o is almost always long.

~ō▣e~　　　rōde, hōme, cōre

15.15.15 When ol is followed in the same syllable by d, k, l, st, or t, then the o almost always becomes long. (The "l" sound in olk virtually disappears.)

~ōld~　　　ōld, cōld, mōld
~ōlk~　　　fōlk, yōlk
~ōll~　　　rōll, tōll, knōll, pōll
~ōlst~　　hōlster, bōlster, pōlster
~ōlt~　　　bōlt, cōlt, jōlt

15.15.16 When oll is divided between syllables, the o becomes a short ŏ.

~ŏl◇l~　　　fŏlly, hŏllow, dŏllar, cŏllect

15.15.17 ou has many sounds:
vowel blend "ŏw" (as in "ŏwl"),
long "ō" (as in "cōde"),
long "ōō" = "û" (as in "too" "flû"),
short "ŏŏ" = "ü" (as in "foot" "püt"),
short "ŭ" (as in "blood" "putt").

~ou~	vowel blend ŏw: ŏur, mŏuse, dŏubt
	long ō: pour, soul, shoulder
	long ōō: you, soup, tour, courier
	short ŏŏ: would, should, could, tour
	short ŭ: young, touch, famous, trouble

15.15.18　ough has many sounds:
vowel blend "ŏw" (as in "ŏwl"),
long "ō" (as in "cōde"),
short "ŏ" (as in "cŏd"),
long "ōō" = û (as in "tōō" "flû"),
short "ŏff" (as in "ŏff"),
short "ŭff" (as in "pŭff").

~ough~	vowel blend ŏw: drŏught, dŏughty, bŏugh
	long ō: dough(nut), (al)though, borough, furlough, thorough(bred/fare/going), bough
	short ŏ: ought, bought, (be)sought, nought, (over)wrought, brought, fought, (be/fore/after)thought(ful/less)
	long ōō = û: through(out), slough
	short "ŏff": cough, trough
	short "ŭff": rough(en), tough(en), enough

15.15.19　When ou is followed by r or l, the ou usually has the long "ō" sound.

~ōur~	fōur, pōur, cōurt, sōurce, gōurd
~ōul~	sōul, mōuld, bōulder, pōultry

15.15.20　In many French words, r swallows up the "ou" sound.

~our~	flourish (fl'r-ish), journal (j'r-n'l), courteous (c'r-te-ous)

15.15.21a　ow may say the vowel blend in "ŏwl," especially if followed by d, l, or el, or by an n or er when it is not a verb.

~ŏw~	allŏw, cŏw, hŏw, nŏw, sŏw, vŏw
~ŏwd~	crŏwd, hŏwdy, rŏwdy
~ŏwl~	ŏwl, cŏwl, fŏwl, hŏwl (but bowl)
~ŏwel~	bŏwel, dŏwel, Pŏwell, tŏwel
~ŏwn~	crŏwn, dŏwn, frŏwn, gŏwn, tŏwn
~ŏwer~	flŏwer, shŏwer

15.15.21b **ow** may say the long "ō" sound in "snow," especially if followed by **n** when it is a verb.

~ōw~	blōw, flōw, mōw, snōw, shadōw
~ōwn~	ōwn, mōwn, thrōwn

15.15.22 **oy** forms the vowel blend ōy as in "boy."

~ōy~	ōyster, vōyage, tōy

P

15.16

SOUNDS:
popper

OPENERS:
ph, ph(l/r), pl, pr, sp(l/r), [p]n, [p]s, [p]t

CLOSERS:
lp(s), mp(s), m[p]t(s), (l/r)ph(s), ps, rp(s), sp(s)

15.16.1 Single consonant **p**

~p~	park, keep, soapy

15.16.2 Double consonant **p**

~pp~	popper, appraise, topping

15.16.3 **p** is silent when followed by **b**.

~pb~	cupboard, raspberry, clapboard

15.16.4 When **ph** is in one syllable, it is a Greek spelling for the sound of "f."

~ph~	phosphor, nephew, graph

15.16.5 Consonant blend **pl**

~pl~	plant, splendid, reply

15.16.6 **p** is silent when it is followed in the same syllable by **n**, **s**, or **t**.

◇~pn~◇	pneumatic, pneumonia
◇~ps~◇	psalm, psychic (s also is silent in corps)
◇~pt~◇	ptomaine, prompt, receipt

15.16.7 Consonant blend **pr**.

~pr~	sprocket, represent, praise

Q

15.17

SOUNDS:
Iraq

OPENERS:
qu as in quit, sq as in squaw

CLOSERS:
(r)que(s), quet, sque(s)

15.17.1 Consonant blend **qu** with the sound of "kw"

~qu~	quick, queen, squirrel

15.17.2 **qu**, when followed by short **ă**, usually changes **a** to broad **ä**.

~quä~	quädrant, equäl, squäd (but quăck)

15.17.3 In French words, **qu** sounds like **k**.

~qu~	piquant, antique, mosquito, liquor

R

15.18

SOUNDS:
   roar (voiced),
   rhyme (unvoiced "hr" sound)

OPENERS:
   br, cr, chr, dr, fr, gr, kr, pr, ph(l/r), rh,
   shr, tr, thr, wr

CLOSERS:
   rb(s). rc(s), rd(s), rf(s), rg, rh, rk(s),
   rl(s), rm(s), rn(s), rp(s), rque(s), rs, rsh,
   rt(s/z), rv(es), rz

15.18.1 Single consonant r

~r~	roar, girl, hair

15.18.2 Double consonant r

~rr~	See under: arr, err, irr, orr, urr.

15.18.3 The Greek spelling rh or rrh is properly pronounced without voice, as "hr."

~řh~	řhetoric, řhyme, řhubarb, myrřh

15.18.4 When r is pronounced after a long vowel, especially after long ī or long ū, the sound of consonantal "y" or "w" often appears, creating a semi-syllable (y'r, w'r).

~◉r~	mare (mā-y'r), mere (mē-y'r), mire (mī-y'r), more (mō-w'r), mure (myū-w'r)

15.18.5 r alters the sound of short ă to broad ä. (See also 15.1.15-16.)

~är~	fär, jär, lärk, lärge, scärlet, härvest

15.18.6 r alters the sound of short ŏ to long ō. (See also 15.15.12-13.)

~ōr~	ōr, cōrn, stōrm, fōrtify

15.18.7　　r tends to swallow up the sound of short vowels
　　　　　ĕ, ĭ, and ŭ.

~ĕr~	person (p'r-son), service (s'r-vice)
~ĭr~	dirt (d'rt), stir (st'r)
~ŭr~	nurse (n'rse), purchase (p'r-chase)

15.18.8　　When the French spelling re occurs at a word's
　　　　　end, the syllable is pronounced as if spelled ĕr,
　　　　　and the r swallows the short "ĕ" sound.

~re◆	acre, ogre, lucre, timbre, massacre, mediocre

S

SOUNDS:
　so (unvoiced "s" sound),
　is (voiced "z" sound)

OPENERS:

15.19
　[p]s, sc, sch(l/m/n/r/w), sh(r), si, sk, sl,
　sm, sn, sp(l/r), squ, st(r), su(a/e/i), sw

CLOSERS:
　(l/r)bs, cks, (l/r)cs, (l/r)ds, (l/r)fs,
　(l/r)gs, (l/r)ks, (r)ls, (l/r)ms, ng(s), ns,
　(l/r)ps, rs(t), rt(s), sc(s), (r)sh, sk(s),
　sle(s), sm(s), sp(s), sque(s), (l/r)st(s),
　(l/r)ts, tsch, (l/r)ves

15.19.1　　When beginning a word, s never has the voiced
　　　　　"z" sound.

◆s~	sage, see, sift, soft, sun, stun

15.19.2a　s is usually not voiced after a short vowel.

~ŏˇs~	ăsk, rĕsted, blĭster, cŏst, focŭs (but as, is)

15.19.2b　s is usually voiced ("z") after a long vowel.

~ōˉs~	rāise, ēase, rīse, rōse, clōse (verb), rūse (but cease, close (adjective))

15.19.2c   s is usually voiced ("z") after a vowel at the end of a word.

~⊙s♦	is, as, has, goes, series, skies, (but gas, yes, this, us)

15.19.3a   s or es at the end of a word is not voiced after an unvoiced consonant (hard c, f, k, p, ph, qu, t, soft th).

~▣s♦	arcs, puffs, works, tops, graphs, goats, baths
~▣es♦	fifes, bakes, drapes, antiques, dates

15.19.3b   s or es at the end of a word usually has the voiced "z" sound after a voiced consonant (b, d, g, l, m, n, r, hard th, v, w, y).

~▣s♦	bobs, bids, bags, dolls, hums, tons, flowers, flows, stays
~▣es♦	blades, dales, frames, bathes, stoves

15.19.4   s is not voiced when blended with an unvoiced consonant mute (hard c, ch, k, p, ph, t).

~◇s▣~	scare, discard, schedule, schizo-, skill, ask, spell, despise, sphere, still, monster

15.19.5   s is not voiced when blended with a voiced consonant semi-vowel (l, m, n, w, and u as "w").

~◇s▣~	slow, small, snail, swim, suede

15.19.6   s is not voiced when it is part of a triple consonant blend at the beginning of a syllable.

~◇s▣▣~	scrub, describe, split, spring, squash, string, restrict

15.19.7   s has the voiced "z" sound when followed by a b or an m, except sm at the beginning of a word.

~⊙sb~	husband, presbyterian
~⊙sm~	baptismal, charismatic

15.19.8 At the end of a word, sm forms a semi-syllable (z'm).

~⊙sm♦	prism (pri-z'm), spasm (spa-z'm)

15.19.9 ss is almost always preceded by a short vowel, and is never voiced.

~ŏss~	păss, chĕss, kĭss, tŏss, fŭss
	(but long vowel: bāss, grōss)
	(but voiced: dessert)
	(but "zh" sound: fissure)
	(but "sh" sound: issue. See 15.19.13b.)

15.19.10 s is not voiced before a soft c which precedes e, i, or y.

~sce~	scent, descend, scion, disciple, scythe
	(but sceptic)

15.19.11 s is usually not voiced when it follows a consonant and precedes silent e.

~▣se◇	else, horse, expense, collapse

15.19.12 s is sometimes voiced in verbs after two vowels and before silent e.

~⊙⊙se◇	praise, pause, please, choose, rouse, nauseate
	(but adjective: nauseous; nouns: grease, geese, goose, mouse)

15.19.13 At the beginning or the ending of a word, sh always has the "sh" sound.

♦sh~	she, ship, short
~sh♦	hush, marsh, English

15.19.14   si has the voiced "zh" sound between vowels,
and the unvoiced "sh" sound after a consonant
(including another s).

~◉si◉~	vision, explosion, fusion
~▫si~	mansion, controversial (but version)
~ssi~	passion, session, mission (but fission)

15.19.15a   su usually has the voiced "zh" sound between
vowels or between a vowel and r.

~◉su◉~	leisure, casual, usual
~◉sur~	measure, closure

15.19.15b   su usually has the unvoiced "sh" sound when beginning a word, or after a consonant (including
another s).

◆su~	sure, sugar
~▫su~	issue, insure (but fissure)

15.19.16   In many French words, final s is silent.

~s◆	apropos, bourgeois, chamois, chassis, corps, debris

T

15.20

SOUNDS:
  totter
OPENERS:
  [p]t, st(r), th(r), ti, tr, tw
CLOSERS:
  [b]t(s), [c]t(s), ft(s), lt(s/z), m[p]t(s),
  nt(s), rt(s/z), (l/r)st(s), tch, (l/r)th(s),
  tsch, ts, tz, xt(s)

15.20.1   Single consonant t

~t~	tot, party, altar, cobalt

15.20.2   Double consonant t

~tt~	totter, batter

15.20.3a In many French words, final t is silent.

~t♦	beret, buffet, ballet

15.20.3b In French words with a final e after t, the t is
not silent.

~te♦	route, suite, elite, gazette, silhouette

15.20.4 tch makes the same sound as soft ch in "church."

♦~◉tch~	ditch, watched, butcher

15.20.5a When th is a blend (as in thorn), and not
divided between syllables (as in hothead), it is
not voiced at the beginning of nouns, verbs, and
adjectives, nor between vowels in Greek words.

♦th~◇	thorn, think, thin
◇~◉th◉~◇	athlete, ether, ethic

15.20.5b th is voiced at the beginning of pointing words,
and between vowels in English words.

♦th~◇	the, this, that, there
◇~◉th◉~◇	either, clothe, bathe

15.20.6 When a word ends with an unvoiced th, and
an e is added to form a verb, or an s is added
to form a plural or a verb form, then th will
change to voiced.

~the♦	cloth-clothe, bath-bathe, lath-lathe
~ths♦	bath-baths, mouth-mouths, booth-booths
	(but silent th: clothes)

15.20.7 th has the "t" sound in some names and foreign
words.

| ~th~ | Thomas, Beethoven, thyme |

15.20.8 th is silent when preceded by an s.

| ~sth~ | isthmus, asthma |

15.20.9 When thr or thw is not divided between syllables, it is not voiced.

| ~thr~ | three, threat, thread |
| ~thw~ | thwart |

15.20.10a ti at the beginning of a word says hard "t" sound.

| ◆ti~ | title, tiny, tight |

15.20.10b ti within a word says the unvoiced "sh" sound when it is followed by a vowel.

| ~ti◉~ | ratio, nation, initial, action, function |

15.20.10c ti within a word says the soft "ch" sound when it follows an s and precedes a vowel.

| ~s◇ti◉~ | Christian, question, bastion |

15.20.11a t in tu says "t" at the beginning of a word.

15.20.11b tu within a word says soft "ch" (as in chair).

| ◆tu~ | tub, turn, tune, tulip |
| ~tu~ | nature, culture, gesture, virtue, actual |

15.20.12 Consonant blend tr

| ~tr~ | tray, contract, extra |

15.20.13 Consonant blend tw

| ~tw~ | twice, between, twelve |

15.20.14 t is often not pronounced when preceded by s and followed by le or en.

~stle♦	apostle, hustle, whistle, thistle
~sten♦	hasten, fasten, listen

15.20.15   Consonant blend str

~str~	straw, construct, lustre

U

15.21

SOUNDS:
repūte ("y" with long "ōō" sound),
lûcid (=long "ōō" sound), pŭtt,
püt (=short "ŏŏ" sound),
sŭave (consonantal "w" sound)

DIPHTHONGS:
hạ̈ul, fẹụd, ọ̈ut

COMBINATIONS:
au, augh, eou, ou, ough, ue, uoi(s),
ug, ugh, uh, ui, uoy, uu, uy

OPENERS:
su(a/e/i), (s)qu, ua, ue, ui, uo, uoi,
wu, yu, you

CLOSERS:
(s)que(s)

15.21.1   Long ū says its name, "yōō" (the same as the word "you"). u is long in a syllable which ends in u.

~ū◇~	ūniform, hūmor, fūry, cūrious, būgle

15.21.2   The pronunciation of the consonantal y of the long "ū" ("yōō") sound is swallowed up after the dental mutes d and t, and after the semi-vowels l, r, s, z, and after the "sh," "zh," and soft "ch" sounds, because it is phonetically difficult.

~dû◊~	dûty (not dyōō-ty, but dōō-ty)
~tû◊~	tûlip, tûna
~lû◊~	blûish, lûbricate, lûcid, lûte
~rû◊~	rûin, crûel
~sû◊~	sûgar, casûal
~zû~	azûre
~chû~	chûrch

15.21.3   u is always long when followed by a consonant and a silent e.

~ū▣e◊~	with consonantal y: cūbe, pūre, fūme, hūge
~û▣e◊~	with no consonantal y: sûre, dûke, assûme

15.21.4a   ue at the end of a primitive word always says long "ū."

~ūe◆	with consonantal y: rescūe, statūe, hūe
~ûe◆	with no consonantal y: sûe, dûe, flûe

15.21.4b   ue is silent in French words where ue follows g or q.

~gue◆	tongue, plague, dialogue, rogue (but argue)
~que◆	critique, opaque, clique

15.21.5a   ui says long "ū."

◊~ūi~	with consonantal y: jūice
◊~ûi~	with no consonantal y: sûit, brûise, frûit (but suite pronounced like "sweet")

15.21.5b   ui says short "i" or long "i" in French words where it follows g or q. (u keeps the i from making g soft).

◊gui~	guilt, guide
◊qui~	quit, quite

15.21.6 u is short in a syllable which ends in a consonant.

~ŭ▣◇	(short "ŭ" sound) ŭgly, pŭtt, hŭnted, crŭtch (short "ŏŏ" sound) püt, pülley,
~ü▣◇	pülpit

15.21.7 r swallows up the short "ŭ" sound.

~ŭr~	burnt (b'rnt), turtle (t'r-tle), surprise (s'r-prise)
~ŭrr~	hurrah (h'r-rah), curr (c'rr), furry (f'r-ry)

15.21.8 When u is preceded by a consonant, and followed by a vowel (except another u), all in the same syllable, u has the consonantal "w" sound.

◇▣ŭ◉~◇	sŭave, sŭede, sŭite, qŭote, angŭish

15.21.9 Doubled u may be pronounced as the long ū (yōō) or as two syllables (yōō-ü)

~ūu~	vacuum (văk-yōōm)
~ūü~	continuum (kŭn-tĭn-yōō-üm)

15.21.10 u before a short ă changes a to a broad ä.

~uä~	suäve, squäsh, quärter (but quăck)

V

SOUNDS:
  valve
CLOSERS:
  ves, lv(es), rv(es)

15.22

15.22.1 Consonant v

~v~	vine, advance, provision

15.22.2a At the end of a word, v is always followed by silent e.

15.22.2b A single vowel before ve is almost always short.

| ~ve♦ | greave, groove, relieve, solve |
| ~ŏve♦ | give, have, love, move (but ēve) |

W

SOUNDS:
watt (voiced), what (unvoiced "hw")

DIPHTHONGS:
āwe, few, ŏwl, ōwe

15.23

OPENERS:
dw, sw, tw, wa, we, wea, wh, wha, whe, whea, whi, who, why, wi, wo, wr, wu, wy, zw

15.23.1 w followed by a vowel is always voiced.

| ~w◉~ | wagon, aware, entwine |

15.23.2 w usually changes short ă to broad ä.

| ~wä~ | wänd, swän, wället (but wăck) |

15.23.3 r changes broad ä after w to long "ō" sound.

| ~war~ | war, warning, dwarf, swarm, ward |

15.23.4 w followed by h in the same syllable is not voiced (properly pronounced "hw").

| ◇wh~◇ | what, whether, anywhere |

15.23.5 Because o swallows the "w" sound in the pronunciation of "hw," the letters who are pronounced "hō" or "hōō."

| ~who~ | whole, whore
who, whom, whose |

15.23.6 w changes short ŏ to the short "ŭ" sound (as in "pŭtt" or "püt").

| ~wo~ | won, wonder
wolf, woman |

15.23.7   r swallows the short "ŭ" sound of o after w.

| ~wor~ | word (w'rd), worst (w'rst) worship (w'rship) |

15.23.8   r completely swallows the "w" sound, making w silent.

| ◆wr~ | write, wrong, wreckage |

15.23.9   In some words, we do not pronounce the w because of the phonetic complexity.

| ~w~ | two, answer, sword |

X

SOUNDS:
 box
CLOSERS:
 nx, xt

15.24

15.24.1   Unvoiced x (double letter "ks" sound) always appears at the end of a syllable.

| ~x◇ | fox, mixing, sixteen |

15.24.2   Voiced x ("gz" sound) appears when the syllable with the x is not stressed and the next syllable begins with a vowel sound.

| ~◉x◇◉~ | exact (eg-zakt), auxiliary (aug-zil-yary), exhort (eg-zort – silent h) |

15.24.3   Voiced x ("gz" sound) appears at the beginning of a Greek word, but the hard "g" sound is phonetically dropped, leaving only the "z" sound.

◆x~   Xerox (ze-rox), Xerxes (zerg-zez),
          xylophone (zy-lo-phone),
          xenophobia (ze-no-pho-bi-ya)

Y

15.25

SOUNDS:
   yam (consonantal "y" sound),
   whȳ (long "ī" sound),
   gy̆m (short "ĭ" sound),
   babŷ (long "ē" sound),
   [y often says whatever i would say.]
DIPHTHONGS:
   hāy, aye, hey, eye, boy
COMBINATIONS:
   ay, ey, uoy, uy
OPENERS:
   why, wy, ya, ye, yea, yo, you, yu

15.25.1   Only when y is at the beginning of a syllable does it say the consonantal "y" sound.

~◇y◉~   yarn, sawyer, canyon, yoyo

15.25.2   y has the long "ī" sound when y follows a consonant at the end of either a stressed syllable or a primitive word.

~▣ȳ◇   cȳclone, tȳrant, stȳlish, crȳ, trȳing, multiplȳ

15.25.3   y or ey has the long "ē" sound in an unstressed suffix at the end of a primitive word.

~▣ŷ◆   babŷ, nearlŷ, countrŷ, ponŷ
~eŷ◆   moneŷ, phoneŷ, honeŷ

15.25.4   ey often says long "ā" in a stressed syllable.

~êy~   hêy, obêy, convêyance

15.25.5   y has the short "ĭ" sound when followed by a consonant in the same syllable.

| ~y̆▣◇ | mȳth, sy̆mbol, gy̆psy |

15.25.6 When a word ends with **ye**, or with **y** followed by a consonant and silent **e**, the **y** says the long "ī" sound.

| ~ȳe♦ | bȳe, dȳe, lȳe, rȳe |
| ~ȳ▣e♦ | tȳpe, stȳle, lȳre, enzȳme |

15.25.7a At the end of a word, or when the next syllable begins with a consonant, **r** swallows the short "ĭ" sound of **y**.

| ~yr♦ | martyr (mar-t'r), satyr (sa-t'r), zephyr (ze-ph'r) |
| ~yr◇▣ | myrtle (m'r-t'l) |

15.25.7b When **yr** is followed by a vowel, that vowel often captures the "r" sound, and the short "ĭ" sound of **y** is heard.

| ~y̆r◉~ | sy̆rup, ly̆ric, py̆ramid, ty̆ranny (but martyrology) |

Z

SOUNDS:
zoo

OPENERS:
[c]z, zh, zi, zw

15.26

CLOSERS:
dz, lz, ltz, nz, rz, rtz, tz

15.26.1 Single consonant **z**

| ~z~ | zipper, frozen, recognize |

15.26.2 When **z** is preceded by **t** in the same syllable, it is not voiced (unvoiced "ts" sound).

| ~tz~ | waltz, quartz, chintz |

15.26.3   zh has the "zh" sound in words derived from Russian, the "j" sound in words derived from Chinese.

~zh~	Zhukov (zhōō-kŏv)
	Zhanjiang (jän-jyäng)

15.26.4   When z is followed by i or u, it changes to the voiced "zh" sound.

~zi~	glazier, brazier
~zu~	azure

15.26.5   z never stands alone at the end of a word. Either silent e or another z is used.

~ze♦	sneeze, bronze, seize
~zz♦	buzz, jazz, fizz, fuzz
	(but quiz, whiz)

Appendices
GAMES AND HOMOPHONE LIST

16. Spelling & Phonics Games

16.1 Spelling Bee Game

Read a spelling rule, then go around from person to person, each person spelling one word per turn. (You may wish to place time limits on each person's turn.) Each player gains one point for each word he says which illustrates the spelling rule which was read, and two points for each word he says which is an exception to the spelling rule.

A person drops out of the round when he cannot think of a word, or when he has misspelled a word. (You may wish to assign a particular dictionary as the judge.)

Continue the round until only one person is left with a word or an exception. Then begin a new round with a new spelling rule.

If someone catches a misspelled word, the catcher gains the point and the misspeller drops out. Persons who have dropped out of the round can still catch wrong spellings and gain points.

Play for a certain amount of time, a certain number of spelling rules, or to a certain point total.

16.2   Letter Chain Game

You are trying to forge a "chain" of letters on the way to spelling a word. Someone begins with a letter. Each person adds a letter to the "letter chain" as the turn passes from person to person. For example, let us say that the first letter chosen is t. The next person could add r, which could begin to spell tree, tractor, trespass or whatever, or he could add h, which could begin to spell the, thought, theory, or whatever. The object is to make the chain as long as you can, or to end the chain on your turn so the next person cannot add another letter, or at least to keep the chain from ending on the turn before your own.

If a person is incapable of adding a letter, he drops out, and the next person in turn begins a new "letter chain" with a new letter.

Only the person whose turn comes next can challenge the last letter added to the "letter chain." When challenged, the person who added the letter to the "letter chain" must say what word he intended to spell. If he fails – either because he was bluffing, or because he has misspelled the word – he drops out, and the next person in turn begins a new word.

The game continues until only one person is left.

Variation: a person gains one point each time he cannot add a letter, or is caught misspelling or bluffing, but he continues in the game until he has too many points – say five points.

16.3   Phonetic Spelling Bee Game

A round begins when one player says a word out loud – it could even be a nonsense word. The other players attempt, in turn, to spell the word any way they can – one spelling per player per turn. [e.g. garfoil, garfoyl, gearfoil (cf. ea in heart), gharfoyl (cf. gh in ghost) etc.] Each player gains one point for each way he spells the word.

A player drops out of the round when he cannot think of another spelling. The round ends when the last person left cannot think of another spelling. Then the next person says another word out loud, and the others attempt in turn to spell the word.

If someone challenges a spelling, the speller must defend the spelling from the phonics rules or by giving an example of the spelling of the sounds from actual English words. If he successfully defends the spelling, he gains the point. If he does not successfully defend the spelling, he does not gain the point, but the challenger gains two points.

Play for a certain time period, to a certain point total, or for a certain number of rounds.

17. Homophones

Homophones are words which are pronounced the same, but are spelled differently. Many of these could also be classified as Anamixonyms (see Section 10.3 Confused Word Pairs). An asterisk (*) marks words with alternate pronunciations. Parentheses ( ) enclose letters which could be added to form more homophones. Brackets [ ] enclose an alternate spelling of the previous word.

acts—ax
ad(s)—add(s)—adze
ade—aid—aide
adieu—ado
adolescence—adolescents
aerie—[eyrie]—airy—eerie
aero—arrow
ail—ale
air—âre—ere—err—e'er—
    Eyre—heir
aisle—I'll—isle
ait—[eyot]—ate—eight
albumen—albumin
all—awl
allowed—aloud
altar—alter
an—Ann
ant—aunt
ante—auntie
appose—oppose
arc—ark
ascent—assent
auger—augur
aught—ought
aural—oral
auricle—oracle
away—aweigh
awed—odd
awful—offal
axel—axle
aye—[ay]—eye—I
bail—bale—bay'll
bailed—baled
bailee—bailey—bailie
bailer—bailor—baler
bailing—baling
bait—bate
baited—bated

baiting—bating
baize—bays—beys
bald—balled—bawled
ball—bawl
band—banned
bard—barred
bare—bear
bark—barque
baron—barren
Barry—berry—bury
basal—basil
base—bass*
based—baste
bases—basis—basses
bask—basque
bat—batt
baud—bawd
bay—bey
be—bee
beach—beech
bean—been*
beat—beet
beau—bow
beaut—butte
been*—bin
been*—Ben
beer—bier
bel—Bel—bell—belle
bends—Ben's
berth—birth
besot—besought
better—bettor
bight—bite—byte
billed—build
bit—bitt
blew—blue
bloc—block
boar—Boer—boor—bore

board—bored
boarder—border
bode—bowed
bold—bowled
bolder—boulder
bole—boll—bowl
boos—booze
born—borne—bourn—bourne
borough—burro—burrow
bough—bow
bouy—boy
bra—braw
brae—bray
braid—brayed
braise—brays—braze
brake—break
breach—breech
bread—bred
brewed—brood
brews—bruise
bridal—bridle
broach—brooch
broom—brougham
brows—browse
bundt—bunt
bur—burr
burger—burgher
bus—buss
bussed—bust
but—butt
buy—by—bye
buyer—byre
cache—cash
cached—cashed
calendar—calender
call—caul—col
caller—choler—collar
can't—cant
cannon—canon
canter—cantor
canvas—canvass
capital—capitol
carat—caret—carrot—karat
carol—carrel
carpal—carpel
cast—caste
caster—castor
caught—cot
cause—caws
cay—key—quay
cedar—seeder
cede—seed
ceding—seeding

ceiling—sealing
cell—sell
cellar—seller
censer—censor—sensor
census—senses*
cent—scent—sent
cents—scents—sense
cere—sear—seer*—sere
cereal—serial
Ceres—series
cession—session
chalk—chock
chance—chants
chard—charred
chased—chaste
check—cheque—Czech
checker—chequer
cheap—cheep
chews—choos—choose
Chile—chili—chilly
choir—quire
choral—coral
chorale—corral
chord—cord—cored
chute—shoot
cider—sider
cite(s/ed)—sight(s/ed)—
    site(s/ed)
clack—claque
Claus—clause—claws
clew—clue
click—clique
climb—clime
close—clothes
coal—cole
coaled—cold
coarse—course
coat—cote
coax—cokes
cocks—cox—Cox
coddling—codling
coffer—cougher
coign—[quoin]—coin
colonel—kernel
complacence—complaisance
complacent—complaisant
complement*—compliment
conch—conk
coo—coup
coolie—coolly
copes—copse
copped—copt
cops—copse

core—corps
cosign—cosine
council—counsel
cousin—cozen
craft—kraft
crater—krater
creak—creek
crewed—crude
crewel—cruel
crews—cruise
cue—Kew—queue
currant—current
curser—cursor
cygnet—signet
cymbal—symbol
dam(med)—damn(ed)
days—daze
dear—deer
dependence—dependents
deviser—devisor
dew(s)—do(s)—due(s)
die(d/s)—dye(d/s)
dine—dyne
dire—dyer
disc—disk
discreet—discrete
discussed—disgust
do—doe—dough
doc—dock
does—doughs—doze
done—dun
dos—dues
douse—dowse
draft—draught
dual—duel
earn—erne—[ern]—urn
eery—Erie—eyrie
elicit—illicit
elude—illude
epic—epoch
eunuchs—Unix
ewe—yew—you—u
ewes—use—yews
eyelet—islet
facts—fax
fain—feign
faint—feint
fair—fare
fairing—faring
fairy—ferry
faker—fakir
farrow—pharoah
fate—fête

faun—fawn
faux—foe
fay—Faye—fey
fays—faze—phase
faze(d/s)—phase(d/s)
feat—feet
ferrate—ferret
ferrule—ferule
feted—fetid
few—phew
fie—phi
file—phial
fills—fils
filter—philter
find—fined
finish—Finnish
fir—fur—furr
fisher—fissure*
fizz—phiz
flair—flare
flea—flee
flecks—flex
flew—flu—flue
Flo—floe—flow
flocks—phlox
floe(s)—flow(s)
floor—fluor
flour—flower
foaled—fold
for—fore—four
forego—forgo
foreword—forward
fort—forte
forth—fourth
foul—fowl
franc—frank
frees—freeze—frieze
friar—fryer
furs—furze
gaff—gaffe
gage—gauge
gait—gate
gaited—gated
galipot—gallipot
galley—gally
gallop—galop
gamble—gambol
gays—gaze
gene(s)—jean(s)
gibe—jibe
gild—gilled—guild
gilt—guilt
gin—jinn

gnawed—nod
gneiss—nice
gnu(s)—knew—new(s)—nu
gored—gourd
gorilla—guerrilla
grade—grayed
graft—graphed
grate—great
grays—graze
grease—Greece
greave(s)—grieve(s)
grill—grille
grisly—grizzly
groan—grown
guessed—guest
guide—guyed
guise—guys
gunnel—gunwale
gym—Jim
ha—[hah]—haw
hail—hale
hair—hare
hairy—Harry—harry
hall—haul
halve(s)—have(s)
hammock—hummock
hangar—hanger
Harold—herald
hart—heart
haut—ho—hoe
hay—hey
hays—haze
heal—heel—he'll
he'd—heed
he'll—hill
hear—here
heard—herd
heigh—hi—hie—high
heroin—heroine
hew—hue—Hugh
hide—hied
higher—hire
him—hymn
hoar—hoer—whore
hoard—horde—whored
hoarse—horse
hoes—hose
hold—holed
hole—whole
holey—holy—wholly
hostel—hostile
hour(s)—our(s)
Howell—howl

humerus—humorous
idle—idol—idyll—[idyl]
ileum—ilium
in—inn
inc—ink
incidence—incidents
incite—insight*
indict—indite
innocence—innocents
inns—ins
instance—instants
it's—its
jam—jamb
jewel—joule
juggler—jugular*
key—quay
knap—nap
knave—nave
knee—nee*
knead—kneed—need
knickers—nickers
knight—night
knit—nit
knits—nits
knob—nob
knock—nock
knot(ty)—naught(y)—
   [nought(y)]—not
know—no
knower—nor
knows—noes—nose
laager—lager
lac—lack
lacks—lax
lade—laid
lain—lane
lair—layer*
lam—lamb
lay—lea—[ley]—lei
lays—lase—laze—leas—[leys]—
   leis
lea—lee—li
leach—leech
lead—led
leak—leek
lean—lien
leas—lees
leased—least
lends—lens
lessen—lesson
levee—levy
liar—lyre

lichen—liken
lie—lye
lieu—loo—Lou
lightening—lightning
limb—limn
limbs—limns
links—lynx
literal—littoral
lo—low
load—lode—lowed
loath—loathe
loan—lone
loch—lock
lochs—locks—lox
loon—lune
loop—loupe
loos*—lose
loot—lute
lord—lowered
lore—lower
lumbar*—lumber
mach—mock
made—maid
mail—male
main—mane
maize—maze
mall—maul—moll
manner—manor
mantel—mantle
marc—mark—marque
mare—mayor
marquee—marquis
marry—Mary—merry
marshal—Marshall—martial
mask—masque
massed—mast
Mays—maze
me—mi
mean—mien
meat—meet—mete
meter—metre
medal—meddle
men's—mends
metal—mettle
mewl—mule
mews—muse
might—mite
mince—mints
mind—mined
miner—minor
missal—missile
missed—mist
misses—Mrs.

moan—mown
moat—mote
mode—mowed
moire—moray*
moo—moue
mood—mooed
moor—more—mower
moose—mousse
moral—morel
morn—mourn
morning—mourning
muscle(s)—mussel(s)
mussed—must
mustard—mustered
naval—navel
nay(s)—nee*—neigh(s)
nays—neighs
neap—neep
nigh—nye
none—nun
oar—or—ore—o'er
od—odd
oh(s)—owe(s)
one—won—Juan*
oohs—ooze
ordinance—ordnance
overdo—overdue
p—pea
pa—paw
paced—paste
packed—pact
packs—pax
pail—pale
pain—pane
pair—pare—payer—pear
palate—palette—pallet—pal-
lette
pall—Paul—pawl
pa's—pause—paws
pascal—paschal
passed—past
patience—patients
paten—[patin]—patten
peace—piece
peak—peek—peke—pique
peal(ed/s)—peel(ed/s)
pearl—purl
pedal—peddle—petal*
peer—pier
pencil—pensil
per—purr
petit—petty
pi—pie—pye

pica—pika
picnic—pyknic
pieced—piste
pincer—pincher—pinscher
pistil—pistol
picks—pyx—[pix]
place—plaice
plain—plane
plait—plate
planar—planer
pleas—please
pleural—plural
plum—plumb
pocks—pox
polar—poler
Pole—pole—poll
poled—polled
pone—pony
poof—pouffe—[pouf]
poor—pore—pour
popery—potpourri*
praise—prays—preys
pray—prey
precedence—precedents—
  presidents*
premier—premiere
presence—presents
pride—pryed
pries—prize
prince—prints
principal—principle
profit—prophet
pros—prose
psalter—salter
psi*—sigh
quarts—quartz
quean—queen
quince—quints
rabbet—rabbit
rack—wrack
racket—racquet
rain—reign—rein
raise—rays—raze
rap—wrap
rapped—rapt—wrapped
ray—re
read—red
read—rede—reed
reading—reeding
reads—reeds
real—reel
recede—reseed
reck—wreck

reek—wreak
resinate—resonate
resisters—resistors
rest—wrest
retch—wretch
review—revue
rheum—room
rheumy—roomie—roomy
rho—roe—row
rhumb—rum
rhyme—rime
rigger—rigor
right—rite—wright—write
ring—wring
rise—ryes
road—rode—rowed
roam—Rome
roar—rower
roil—royal
role—roll
'roo—roux—rue
rood—rude
roomer—rumor
root—route*
rose—rows
rot—wrought
rote—wrote
rough—ruff
rout—route*
rude—rued
rye—wry
sachet—sashay
sacks—sax
sail—sale
sane(r)—seine(r)
saver—savor*
sawed—sod
scene—seen
scull—skull
sea—see—si—c
seal—seel
seam(s)—seem(s)
seamen—semen*
sear—seer—sere—cere*
seas—sees—seize
sects—sex
seek—Sikh
serf—surf
serge—surge
sew—so—sol—sow
sewer*—soar—sower
sewer*—suer
shake—sheikh—[sheik]

shall—shell*
she'll—shill
shear(s)—sheer(s)
sheave—shiv
shoe(s)—shoo(s)
shone—shown
shore—sure*
sic—sick
sics—six
side—sighed
sighs—size
sign—sine
sink—synch
Sioux—sou—sough—sue—Sue
slay—sleigh
sleight—slight
slew—slough—slue
sloe—slow
soar—sore—sower
soared—sword
solace—soulless
sole—soul
some—sum
son(ny)—sun(ny)
soot—suit*
sordid—sorted*
spade—spayed
spoor—spore
staid—stayed
stair—stare—stayer*
stake—steak
statice—status
stationary—stationery
steal—steel
step—steppe
stile—style
stoop—stoup
storey—story
straight—strait
succor—sucker
suede—swayed
suite—sweet
summary—summery
sundae—Sunday
tach—tack
tacks—tax
tail—tale
taler—tailer—tailor—Taylor
taper—tapir
tare—tear
taught—taut—tot
tearer—terror
tea—tee—ti—t

team(ing/s)—teem(ing/s)
tear*—tier
teas—tease—tees
tenner*—tenor
tense—tents
terce—terse
tern—terne—turn
Thai—tie
the*—thee
their—there—they're
threw—through
throe(s)—throw(s)—thorough*
throne—thrown
thyme—time
tic—tick
ticks—tics
tide—tied
tighten—titan*
timber—timbre*
tire—tyer—tyre—Tyre
to—too—two
toad—toed—towed
tore—tower (one who tows)
tocsin(s)—toxin(s)
toe—tow
told—tolled
tole—toll
ton—tun
tongue—tung
toon*—tune
tor—tore
tort—torte
tough—tuff
toughed—tuft
tracked—tract
tray—trey
troop(er/s)—troup(er/s)—
    troupe(ers)
trussed—trust
vail—vale—veil
vain—vane—vein
vary—very
verses—versus
vial—vile—viol
vice—vise
wax—whacks
wade—weighed
wail—wale—whale
wain—wane—Wayne
waist—waste
wait—weight
waive(r/s)—wave(r/s)
Wales—wales—whales

walk(s)—wok(s)
want—wont
war—wore
ward—warred
ware—wear—weigher—where
warn—worn
warrantee—warranty
warship*—worship
wart—wort
wary—wherry
watt—what*
way—weigh—whey
we—wee—oui
weak—week
weal—wheal—wheel—we'll
weald—wheeled—wield
weather—wether—whether*
weave—we've
we'd—weed
weir—we're
weld—welled
we'll—wheel
wen—when
were—we're*—whir
wet—whet
which*—witch
whig*—wig
while*—wile
whiled*—wild
whine*—wine
whined*—wind*—wined
whirled*—world
whirred*—word
whit*—wit
whither*—wither
who's—whose
whoa—woe
why—wye
will—we'll*
wood—would
worst—wurst
y'all—yawl
yack—yak
yoke(s)—yolk(s)
yore—you're—your
you'll—yule